What Would Madame Defarge Knit?

D1262448

WWMDſK?

WHAT WOULD MADAME DEFARGE KNIT?

CREATIONS INSPIRED BY CLASSIC CHARACTERS

EDITED BY HEATHER ORDOVER

COOPERATIVE PRESS
Cleveland, Ohio

Library of Congress Control Number: 2011921220
ISBN 13: 978-0-9792017-5-2
First Edition
Published by Cooperative Press
www.cooperativepress.com

Charts made with Knit Visualizer (knitfoundry.com).

COOPERATIVE PRESS

Senior Editor: Shannon Okey
Technical Editor: Alexandra Virgiel, with additional assistance by Kate Atherley
(on *Cthulhu Waits* sock pattern)

Visit the WWMDfK? website at http://www.wwmdfk.com

FOREWORD

Right about now you might be thinking, "Well, yeah! What *would* Madame Defarge knit?"

The real answer is: no one knows. Dickens didn't give us any details in *A Tale of Two Cities*. He did, however, make it clear that Defarge was keeping a record of the names of the doomed. Nifty, no? And not exactly the stereotype of the granny knitting peacefully in her rocker. No, the good Madame was no pushover. In fact, the penultimate scene in *A Tale of Two Cities* — shortly before Sydney Carton immortalizes himself — is the showdown designed for we-who-love-The-Madame, when she has a knock-down, drag-out, hair-pulling fight with Lucy Manette's nanny.

A knitter, even without needles in hand, can be a formidable character.

And isn't that the way we want it? We love fiction because of the characters: those people who inhabit the pages and then haunt our brains, making us mull or ponder or reflect or question or obsess. And classic literature is full of great characters — some of the greatest ever written. You probably think you know them, even if you haven't read their book: mousy Jane Eyre; the sensitive Creature from *Frankenstein*; independent Jo from *Little Women*; brainy Elizabeth Bennett from *Pride and Prejudice*; striving Pip and the pathetically defiant Miss Havisham from *Great Expectations*; clever Huck Finn and frustrating Tom Sawyer; gawky Ichabod Crane from "The Legend of Sleepy Hollow"; the guilty Dr. Jekyll and the evil Mr. Hyde; poor Hester Prynne from *The Scarlet Letter*; or our own, tougher–than–titanium Madame Defarge.

Each designer who contributed to this book drew inspiration from a character out of classic fiction. Sometimes the choice of project is obvious — such as Madame Defarge's stole, or a Frankenstein chullo hat with knitted neck bolts that actually light up. Sometimes it's not so obvious, as with a purposefully geometric Noro shawl all ready to stage the next Colour Revolt in *Flatland*.

You may decide you just want to knit a pattern and forget about the bookish stuff for now. Fine. We don't judge. But don't be surprised if part of the way through your first pattern you find yourself reading about the writer's inspirational process and what it was about their particular character that drove them to the design. And don't be surprised if you feel an overwhelming urge to go somewhere like Librivox.org and download the whole, lovely book after listening to the designer reading her essay about it.

We've all been there. It's a nice place to live. So, grab your pointy sticks of choice, plug in a good book, and settle in to our happy little corner of the knitting world.

TABLE OF CONTENTS

PREFACE

To say this book has been a labor of love misses the mark by a few thousand miles.

Everything about this has come from a warm, fuzzy place — from CraftLit which started the whole thing in 2006, to my designer friends who have provided the bounty you see here, to my family who thought this was the niftiest thing ever. It makes me proud and happy to be able to pass it on to you in hopes that you'll find voices that sound like old friends, insights that spark your own imagination and creativity, and patterns (or recipes) that make you want to go out and do brave things yourself.

From me and all the conspirators at *WWMDfK?* — welcome!

Heather Anne Ordover
Tucson, Arizona
February 2011

This book's editor, publisher and contributors remain resolute in their belief that a good skein of cashmere laceweight could very likely have improved Mme. Defarge's mood. Who needs a revolution when you have cashmere to knit?

INTRODUCTION

In compiling and editing this book, we made some decisions that we hope will make it easy and pleasant to use. We also added wraps per inch (WPI) information where we could to facilitate yarn substitution and help our spinner friends.

Our levels of difficulty are expressed visually:

For the Early-in-the-Career Knitter: the freedom (or *liberté*, in French) to embark on the adventure:

For the Brave Beginner or the Intermediate Knitter, a sense of equality (*egalité*) with one's peers:

And for the Expert Knitter or Intermediate-Willing-to-Stick-Out-His-or-Her-Neck-Knitter, a sense of kinship (fraternity, or *fraternité*) with those of us who choose to go out on a limb:

USING THIS BOOK AND FINDING UPDATES

Certain assumptions were made during the creation of this book:

- That you know how to knit
- Or that you know how to crochet.

If you are in neither of these camps, there are marvelous places you can go to on the web that will teach you the following:

- how to knit continental (carrying yarn with the left hand)
- how to knit "English" (throwing yarn with right hand)
- how to crochet

The table of contents is organized thematically by section: What I Did for Love, Song of the Sea, and Women of Valor. Each pattern is preceded by its designer's reflections on the role of their character in the design process, and each section is separated by an interlude — a pattern too unique to be held back by a category.

Resources and links can be found throughout the book. If you are currently reading the ebook version, then links should be live. If you've got the bound version, and would rather not type long URLs, head over to wwmdfk.com — the links will be listed there in their entirety, and will be updated if necessary. The web is fluid and we'd rather not have you get caught in a revolving door of broken links and information.

In addition to its own website, WWMDfK? help can also be found on the CraftLit group on Ravelry. http://www.ravelry.com/groups/craftlit-podcast

The following page contains the text abbreviations used in the patterns. For charting, we use standard Knit Visualizer symbols as much as possible. Please see pages 191-194 for a full key. There is also a Stitch Glossary on page 190 with explanations of several tricky stitches.

WHERE'S THE COLOR?

Because so many knitters use the internet as a source for pattern information, we deliberately chose to print this book in black and white in order to emphasize Jen Minnis' fantastic Victorian-esque "woodcut" illustrations knowing that you, the reader, could go online to see color variations of the projects (whether on the book's website, Ravelry or elsewhere). Keeping production costs down also allows us to pay the contributing designers more for their work!

ABBREVIATIONS

Knitting abbreviations

alt	*alternate*
BO	*bind off*
CO	*cast on*
cont	*continue*
dec	*decrease*
dpn	*double pointed needle*
est	*established*
foll	*follows, following*
inc	*increase*
k	*knit*
k2tog	*knit 2 together*
k3tog	*knit 3 together*
kfb	*knit into front and back of same st*
kwise	*knitwise/as if to knit*
m1	*make 1*
m1l	*make 1 left*
m1p	*make 1 purl*
m1r	*make 1 right*
p	*purl*
p2tog	*purl 2 together*
pm	*place marker*
pwise	*purlwise/as if to purl*
rep	*repeat*
s2kp	*slip 2, knit 1, pass 2 slipped sts over*
sk2p	*slip 1, k2tog, pass slipped st over*
skp	*slip 1, knit 1, pass slipped stitch over*
sl	*slip*
ssk	*sl1 kwise, sl1 kwise, insert left-hand needle into front of these 2 sts, k2tog.*
ssp	*sl1 kwise, sl1 kwise, sl both sts back to left-hand needle, p2tog tbl*
tbl	*through the back loop*
wyib	*with yarn in back*
wyif	*with yarn in front*
yo	*yarn over*

Crochet abbreviations

blo	*back loop only*
ch	*chain*
dc	*double crochet*
fdc	*foundation double crochet*
fhdc	*foundation half double crochet*
flo	*front loop only*
fsc	*foundation single crochet*
hdc	*half double crochet*
sc	*single crochet*
sl st	*slip stitch*
yo	*yarn over hook*

For a full key to all chart symbols used in the book, see page 191.
You can also download a copy from the WWMDfK? website at *wwmdfk.com*

WHAT I DID FOR LOVE

Love is a verb.

Or it *should* be.

We focus on how we feel when we're in love so often that we stop paying attention to what we do. It's easier to see the consequences of this situation when we're reading fiction, whether it's Macon's troubled life in Anne Tyler's *Accidental Tourist*, Scarlett's stubborn resistance to be honest with Rhett (or even with herself), or Victor's obsessive indifference to the things — people and creations — upon which he should be focusing his love.

What follows in this section are patterns drawn from our reflections on characters who are in the throes of love — some happily, mostly fraught, but all passionately. Jane spends much of her time secretly in love (and not-so-secretly in misery). Dorothy is in love with — *it depends on whether you're looking at the book or the film* — home, adventure, friendship — you can go anywhere with Dorothy. And while Tristan and Isolde are doomed lovers, they are lovers nonetheless and they are willing to pay for that love with their lives. It's a tremendously romantic idea — until you're in it yourself.

And that brings us to the darker side of love: obsessive love and the dangers it can pose to the innocent mind. Victor Frankenstein is something of a poster child for obsessive love. First, arguably, is his love for his mother; then for knowledge; then for the power to create life. It doesn't take a Magic 8 ball to know that it will all go badly, and soon. And there's the Creature, poor thing, who only wanted his creator to acknowledge him, care for him, notice him. When he was ignored and vilified, he became obsessed with having Victor create someone for him to spend his life with — obsessed enough to kill. There is poor Bertha, the madwoman in Mr. Rochester's attic, who harkens back to "The Yellow Wallpaper" and serves to further remind us what can happen if we don't pay attention to those who care about us. And there is Dr. Jekyll, the sad, good doctor who is led astray by his Victor-like love of knowledge and his teenage–like belief that he knows better. That nothing will ever go wrong for him.

And lodged at the crossroads between romantic and obsessive love lies Peter Pan. Popular renderings of Peter make his eternal boyhood look fun, but the book is — as one might expect — a bit darker. And so Peter will serve as our interlude between loves. A boy in love with youth, who is unable to grow up — or even to see the benefits of doing so.

Some patterns in this section are whimsical, some are stormy, all will keep you and those you love warm.

Jane's
Ubiquitous Shawl

JANE EYRE
Currer Bell (Charlotte Brontë)

I hurried on my frock and a shawl; I withdrew the bolt, and opened the door with a trembling hand.
- CHAPTER XV

Ah, Jane Eyre! What lonely teenage girl hasn't become lost in this story? As a "woman of a certain age," I laugh at the unrealistic image of marriage represented here, and I rage inside at the controlling, abusive St. John. As a knitter, however, I am fascinated by the use of shawls in the novel. Why? Because at every major turning point of Jane's life, a shawl appears (see page 176). I had anticipated that she would knit, but I was surprised to see shawls used as a literary device.

It shouldn't surprise any of us. We knitters are well-known knitwear spotters in film and TV. We blog about potential nålbinding in *Tristan and Isolde*. We create patterns on our blogs for Mrs. Weasley's sweaters. Why not focus on Ms. Brontë's use of shawls?

In my own life, shawls have become ubiquitous: a lightweight Pashmina comes along in my carryon luggage and makes up for over-enthusiastic air conditioning; a thin shawl covers my shoulders to make me appropriately attired when visiting Italian cathedrals; when I'm especially sad, a shawl is a comforting hug. A pretty shawl can add that certain "something" a plain outfit needs to become stunning (and, worn strategically, can disguise a too-low neckline or a stain on my shirt).

Oh, and when I'm cold, a shawl can keep me warm.

What would Jane Eyre have knit? I believe she would knit a shawl — particularly the one she keeps grabbing in her book. In her day, shawls were practical, everyday items worn for warmth, as well as accessories worn for beauty. Some were triangular, worn crossed over the front and tied in back to enable ease of movement during daily work. Some were long and rectangular, more stole-like, and others were square. Jane was nothing if not practical and (usually) level-headed, so she would want to knit a versatile shawl that was both straightforward to knit and an easily portable project. She was, however, also an artist, and she certainly had a fanciful, romantic side, so Jane's shawl would naturally be pretty.

And so I offer you Jane's Ubiquitous Shawl: versatile because of its square shape, practical because it is knit in the round and is therefore portable and well suited to speed knitting. The sportweight yarn makes this a quick knit, which adds to its practicality, and it's beautiful because, well, don't we all just swoon over lace? Enjoy your knitting and don't leave the house without your shawl!

— Erica

JANE'S UBIQUITOUS SHAWL
Designed by Erica Hernandez

With true "Jane-ian" practicality, this square shawl can easily be customized for different uses: Knit in worsted-weight yarn on size 10 ½ needles, it would be wonderful, big throw (and eat up a metric ton of your stash!); in fingering-weight superwash on size 5 needles, it would be a lovely, special baby gift. Want it smaller? Cut the "Ferns" section in half. Bigger? Expand the center diamond section or the trinity stitch section. Want it fancier? Toss out the picot bind-off and instead knit on some gorgeous lace edging. Hey, if you want, go all out and use laceweight and size 4 needles, expand every section, and add a fancy edging! Jane was an artist; she would have appreciated your creative adaptation of the pattern!

Egalité

FINISHED MEASUREMENTS
52in x 52in [132cm x 132cm]

MATERIALS
- Berroco Ultra Alpaca Light [50% wool, 50% alpaca; 144 yds/131m per 50g skein; 14 WPI], 10 skeins #4207 Salt & Pepper
- Set of five US 7 [4.5mm] double pointed needles US 7 [4.5mm] circular needle, 24in [60cm] long
- 4 locking stitch markers, one a different color from the other three to serve as beg-of-rnd marker

GAUGE
18 sts = 4in [10cm] in stockinette

Take care to knit your first several rounds fairly loosely. If you knit them too tightly, you'll end up with a weird pouch in the center of your shawl, which will not block out.

PATTERN BEGINS
Set-Up Section

Cast on 4 sts, one on each of four dpn, and join for working in the round being careful not to twist. Place beg-of-rnd marker in first stitch. The first few rounds will be very fiddly, but it gets easier quickly.

Rnd 1: Knit.
Rnd 2: Kfb in each stitch. 8 sts.
Rnd 3: Knit.

Before proceeding, place a locking stitch marker on every other stitch, the beg-of-rnd marker counting as the first one. These marked stitches are your four corner stitches where you will make your increases. The corner stitches are marked with a "C" on all charts.

Rnd 4: [K1, yo] eight times. 16 sts.
Rnd 5: Knit.
Rnd 6: [K1, yo, knit to next marked st, yo] four times. 24 sts.
Rnd 7: Knit.

SECTION ONE — DIAMONDS:

"Next day, by noon, I was up and dressed, and sat wrapped in a shawl by the nursery hearth."
— JANE EYRE, CHAPTER III

Why diamonds? I believe the crisp geometric shapes would appeal to Jane's orderly, practical side, plus they remind me of old-fashioned multi-paned windows, where Jane might sit and read. The orderliness of the diamonds also reminds me of the structured life at Lowood. Lastly, I imagine Jane teasing Rochester, something like: "You wish me to wear diamonds? Sir, I already am wearing the diamonds that suit me best; don't you see them here in my shawl?"

Note: You can change to the circular needle whenever you feel you have enough stitches.

Work following Chart A (page 20). Note that only the odd-numbered rounds are charted; knit the even-numbered rounds plain.

After completing Rnd 49 of the chart, you should have 224 sts in total—56 in each quadrant, including corner stitches.

Knit 1 rnd even.

SECTION TWO — TRANSITIONAL LEAVES

"The other articles I made up in a parcel; my purse, containing twenty shillings (it was all I had), I put in my pocket: I tied on my straw bonnet, pinned my shawl, took the parcel and my slippers, which I would not put on yet, and stole from my room."
— JANE EYRE, CHAPTER XXVII

The leaves pointing out from the central diamonds represent the many transitions in Jane's life. The way they point could be said to imply motion, especially the corner leaves, which are more arrow-like.

Work following Chart B (page 21).

After completing Rnd 36 of the chart, you should have 372 sts in total—93 in each quadrant.

SECTION THREE—TRINITY STITCH

"My clothes hung loose on me; for I was much wasted, but I covered deficiencies with a shawl, and once more, clean and respectable looking—no speck of the dirt, no trace of the disorder I so hated, and which seemed so to degrade me, left—I crept down a stone staircase with the aid of the banisters, to a narrow low passage, and found my way presently to the kitchen."
— JANE EYRE, CHAPTER XXIX

Why Trinity Stitch? Many reasons: to represent the Trinity of Jane's faith, which was the basis of her morality; in honor of the good Helen Burns and her faith; for St. John Rivers, whatever we may think of him; lastly in honor of the three love triangles of the book – Jane/Rochester/Bertha, Rochester/Jane/St. John, and Jane/St. John/Miss Oliver.

Work following Chart C (page 20). Both odd- and even-numbered rounds are shown on this chart. The outlined box indicates the pattern repeat.

After completing Rnd 18 of the chart, you should have a total of 444 sts—111 in each quadrant.

SECTION FOUR—FERNS

"I folded my shawl double, and spread it over me for a coverlet; a low, mossy swell was my pillow."
— JANE EYRE, CHAPTER XXVIII

I chose ferns for many reasons: I picture ferns growing on the moor where Jane spent the night under her shawl; I picture ferns in the garden and forest around Thornfield; and I've got a decided weakness for knitted leaves. To me, this stitch pattern looks very lush and makes me think of how unpredictable and complicated Jane's life became. I love how the work is pulled in different directions (like Jane being torn between wanting to be with Rochester and knowing that it would be wrong). When I knit my initial "swatch"—which looks suspiciously like a lap throw—I happened to do it in several complementary colors of stash yarn, and the waviness produced by the leaves was really emphasized in the way the color bands waved.

Work following Chart D (page 20). Only odd-numbered rounds are charted; knit the even-numbered rounds plain. The outlined box indicates the pattern repeat.

You may wonder why each quadrant of the shawl does not come out all nicely mirrored and symmetrical. I did knit one sample this way, but it pulled the yarn in the most unattractive way and I found it to be impossible to block out. This way is asymmetrical, but each quadrant of the shawl is identical, so my personal neuroses are satisfied; I hope yours are, too.

After completing Rnd 57 of the chart, you should have 676 sts in total—169 in each quadrant.

EDGING – PICOT BIND OFF

Rnd 1: Knit.
Rnd 2: [K corner st, yo, k to next marked st, yo] four times. 684 sts.
Bind off as foll: *Using the knitted-on or cable cast on, cast on 2 stitches to left hand needle. Bind off 6 sts (the 2 new stitches plus 4 originals). Repeat from * all the way around the shawl.

FINISHING
Give your shawl a nice bath in a mild wool wash, a quick trip through the spin cycle or a salad spinner, then block the bejabbers out of it. Wear and look tastefully gorgeous, but not flashy. We know Jane would like that.

> **ON THE WWMDFK? WEBSITE:**
>
> *Perhaps a cup of tea and a lovely shortbread while you knit? Let us lead you to proper tea brewing help and a nice shortbread recipe.*

CHART A

CHART D

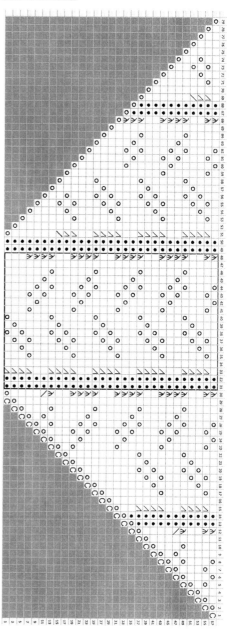

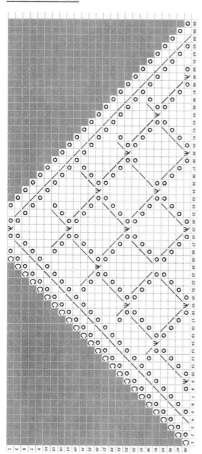

CHART C

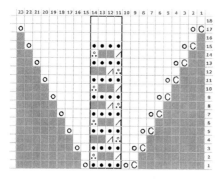

CHART B

Both odd- and even-numbered rounds are shown on this chart.

Chart B corner stitch note: C = Corner knit stitch. This is just a knit stitch. The C is so that you know where you are in the pattern, i.e. if you hit this point, but you're NOT at a corner stitch, you've gone wrong somewhere.

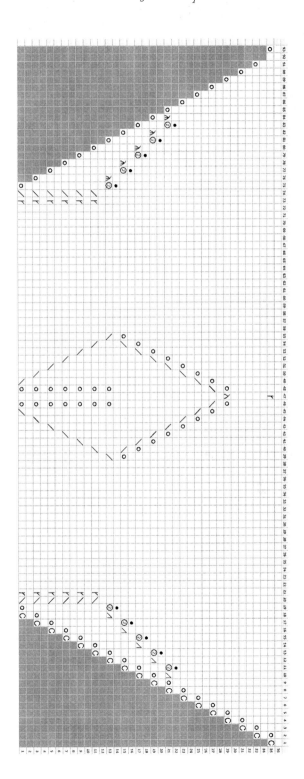

THE OZ SERIES
L. Frank Baum

I am an enormously lucky girl. My parents read to me as a child. Not just a few books, but many. On summer evenings we would lie in the grass and my dad would sit on a large rock in our front yard and read to us. In the cold winter, we would snuggle in our bunk beds, my sister half hanging out of the upper to peek at the pictures of the book in my mom's lap. One of those books took us on a journey to L. Frank Baum's Land of Oz. My memory of the series of 14 books is so vivid — from the mental images the stories themselves made, to glimpsing the embossed pictures on the spines of the old books sitting neat and stylish on a bookshelf. With fabulous illustrations by John R. Neill, these editions have a look that is an amazing representation of early 1900s fashion, especially *Ozma of Oz*, a favorite of my sister's and mine. The book was first printed in 1907 and is third in the series. It's packed with some of the most interesting characters and weirdest stories I have ever encountered in literature. Dorothy's return to Oz contains striking Gibson girl style Princesses, screeching scary Wheelers, Dorothy's close and honorable old friends and new ones, all with amazing adventures and origin stories.

In the middle of this menagerie, is the strange Princess Langwidere:

Now I must explain to you that the Princess Langwidere had thirty heads– as many as there are days in the month. But of course she could only wear one of them at a time, because she had but one neck. These heads were kept in what she called her "cabinet," which was a beautiful dressing room that lay just between Langwidere's sleeping–chamber and the mirrored sitting room.

Each head was in a separate cupboard lined with velvet. The cupboards ran all around the sides of the dressing–room, and had elaborately carved doors with gold numbers on the outside and jewelled–framed mirrors on the inside of them. When the Princess got out of her crystal bed in the morning she went to her cabinet, opened one of the velvet–lined cupboards, and took the head it contained from its golden shelf. Then, by the aid of the mirror inside the open door, she put on the head as neat and straight as could be and after–ward called her maids to robe her for the day.

She ruled for only ten minutes a day. Very tiring indeed! Each head was a switch to a different temperament and look. She was glamorous and terrifying, oozing with arrogance, vapid and uncaring, especially when wearing No.17, which was well known for its temper.

Meeting Dorothy, the Princess sees her as another accessory for her collection:

"You are rather attractive," said the lady, presently. "Not at all beautiful, you understand, but you have a certain style of prettiness that is different from that of any of my thirty heads. So I believe I'll take your head and give you No. 26 for it."

"Well, I b'lieve you won't!" exclaimed Dorothy.

"It will do you no good to refuse," continued the Princess; "for I need your head for my collection, and in the Land of Ev my will is law. I never have cared much for No. 26, and you will find that it is very little worn. Besides, it will do you just as well as the one you're wearing, for all practical purposes."

"I don't know anything about your No. 26, and I don't want to," said Dorothy, firmly. "I'm not used to taking cast-off things, so I'll just keep my own head."

You'll have to read it for yourself to find out what happens.

The interest I had with this character is a bit of a mystery to me. She reminds me of a glossy fashion magazine and a Frankenstein monster all rolled in one. There are other Princesses in the book, frankly better Princesses, namely Ozma — a lovely, benevolent ruler, with a gentle and fair character, calm and soft-spoken. She does good and is loved by all. She is effortlessly stylish, beautiful, and popular. For crying out loud, take a look at that amazing poppy-laden tiara she wears! I should have wanted to be like her. Why then, was I so drawn to this lazy, schizophrenic, ego trip that was Langwidere? Why did I run around the house in my nightgown announcing to each family member I had put on a different head (#17, of course), and was in a foul mood?

Who knows? Maybe it's because this character's priority is something all of us want a bit of sometimes. We want to be able to be selfish, and self-absorbed, to be short, angry, and behave badly. To be able to not be the "us" we feel we have to be. Then just change the head, and change the girl, not worrying about the consequence. She's the opposite of subtle, the opposite of charitable, the opposite of modest — unapologetically so.

She could easily be lumped in with the mean Stepmother in many fairy tales, or any wicked, magic throwing, plot-twisting witch out for revenge and power. But, I think Langwidere is more straightforward, more honest. She'll tell you exactly what she feels and wants. She doesn't care about the power. She is self-absorbed, and has collected many selves to be absorbed in. The rest of the world she gives the least amount of time and thought to. You don't have to like her; I'm not sure I do. I'm sure I wouldn't want to be around her. But maybe just a little, just a tiny bit, I can see the appeal of changing... sometimes... Or maybe I was just jealous of her closet space.

— Gretchen

PRINCESS LANGWIDERE
Designed by Gretchen Funk

What Would Princess Langwidere Knit? Well... not much. I imagine her ordering her poor maid to knit something to cover the join in her neck. I think she would have chosen something soft yet practical. Of course, then she would have changed heads and screamed for a showy lace. The maid, only having had time to make one garment, might cleverly think — Reversible is the trick! Something luxurious and soft to wear with some heads, and smooth and warm for others? Merino and mohair. Done. And then get out of the way because the Princess just might like the look of you!

FINISHED MEASUREMENTS
Circumference: 18in [45.5cm]
Height: 9in [23cm]

Liberté

MATERIALS
- [MC] Aisha Celia Designs Alice Sock Yarn [100% merino wool; 440yd/402m per 100g skein; 15 WPI], 1 skein #175A Olive
- [CC] Crystal Palace Yarns Kid Merino, [25% kid mohair, 28% merino wool, 44% micro nylon; 240yd/219m per 25g skein; 18 WPI], 1 skein #5448 Green
- Two US 3 [3.25mm] circular needles, 16in [40cm] long
- US D [3.25mm] crochet hook for provisional cast on
- Waste yarn
- Stitch marker

GAUGE
28 sts and 34 rows = 4in [10cm] in stockinette with MC

STITCH GUIDE
Lace Pattern (multiple of 9 sts)
Rnd 1 and all odd rnds: Knit.
Rnd 2: *K2, k2tog, yo, k1, yo, ssk, k2; rep from * to end.
Rnd 4: *K1, k2tog, yo, k3, yo, ssk, k1; rep from * to end.
Rnd 6: *K2tog, yo, k5, yo, k2tog; rep from * to end.
Rnd 8: Rep Rnd 6.
Rnd 10: *K3, yo, sl 2, k1, p2sso, yo, k3; rep from * to end.
Rep Rnds 1-10.

PATTERN BEGINS
With waste yarn and using crochet-provisional method (see Glossary, page 192) cast on 126 sts. Join MC leaving a long tail. Knit 1 row, place marker and join to work in the round being careful not to twist.

You'll use the tail of MC left at the beginning to join the inner and outer sides together later, so allow a good 2 yards.

Work in stockinette for 9in [23cm].

Purl 1 rnd.

Cut MC and join CC. Work in Lace Pattern for 9in [23cm], ending with an odd-numbered row.

Cut CC. Now is the time to darn in the ends from joining the mohair—you won't get another chance. So stop and do that now.

Remove the waste yarn from the provisional cast on and place the resulting 126 live stitches on the second circular needle. Hold the two circular needles together, with the MC sts on the front needle and the CC sts on the back needle, wrong sides of the knitting facing each other.

Three-needle BO (see Glossary, page 192) all sts using the MC yarn tail.

Weave in remaining ends, block, smile proudly!

CHART

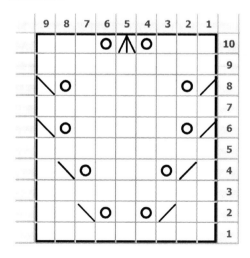

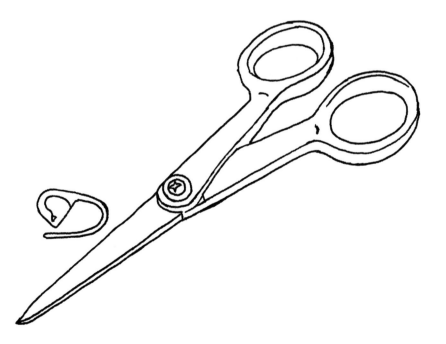

NOT-SO-RUBY SLIPPERS
Designed by Dawn Ellerd

Ruby or not ruby? That is the question. And "NOT" is the shocking answer. The ruby slippers of movie fame are — according to the book — neither ruby nor slippers, but rather innocuous, though powerfully charmed, silver shoes of which the Wicked Witch of the East was rumored to have been rather proud. Like another iconic movie image associated with the story, the seldom-mentioned-in-the-book road of yellow brick, Dorothy's footwear seems to have succumbed to the glamour of Hollywood and suffered a bout of radically inflamed ego.

I've never been able to resolve in my mind just why the shoes needed to be ruby. Is it merely because the city is emerald and the slippers needed to oppose that? They undoubtedly show off better in all of their Technicolor glory, but given the evil inherent in most ruby-hued fairy tale objects, they are the last things I would want to be adventuring about in for days on end. Silver slippers though, seem altogether virtuous — bright and shiny and hopeful — the perfect things to wear heading off to a journey toward your own salvation.

Though I will posit that our good Madame would rather embrace the more arterial hued version, in my head you just cannot have a trip to Oz without the appropriately delightful footwear of your choice. Whether you choose precious metal or gemstone glory, may these slippers enliven your days (or at least keep your toes warm) and forever see you safely home.

— Dawn

SIZE
One size fits most women

FINISHED MEASUREMENTS
Length: 8.25in [21cm] unstretched

MATERIALS
- Cascade 220 Superwash [100% superwash wool; 220 yds/201m per 100g skein; 9 WPI], 1 skein #1946 *or*
- Cascade Fixation [98.3% cotton / 1.7% elastic; 100 yds/91m per 50g skein; 11 WPI], 2 skeins #3611
- US G [4.5mm] crochet hook
- Stitch marker

GAUGE
4.5 sts = 1in [2.5cm] in hdc

PATTERN NOTES

It is very important to use superwash wool or other fiber that will stand up to machine washing and at least a brief tumble in the dryer. The slippers are made with an extreme amount of negative ease so that they hug your foot in good skimmer fashion. As crochet is not as intrinsically elastic as knitting, you will need to periodically wash and dry them to bring them back into optimal foot-hugging proportions.

A word on hdc blo: Because of how it is generated, half double crochet looks like it has a front, middle, and back loop along its top edge. Though it is generally treated like a regular single or double crochet stitch that have those tidy little "V"s along their top, if you work through that extreme back loop only, those "V"s pop out and leave you with a nice little knit stitch detail…and a natural bend point in the fabric.

A few words on sizing: As noted before, these slippers have an extreme amount of negative ease, stretching over your foot to create a "skimmer" type fit. They will accommodate a wide range of shoe sizes. HOWEVER, if you have a particularly small or large foot, I would recommend adding or subtracting four stitches to the foundation row. Foot width should not be as big of an issue, but you can always add a repeat of Row 4 to accommodate a very wide forefoot. Likewise, if you have a significantly narrow foot, you may want to eliminate Row 4.

For instructions on working foundation single crochet, foundation double crochet, etc. (fsc, fdc, fhdc), see Glossary (page 190). In addition, many tutorials for foundation stitches exist to walk you through these techniques. In a nutshell, you are working your chain stitches and first row of stitches at the same time.

PATTERN BEGINS

These slippers are worked in the round, from the center of the sole out and shaped as you go.

Rnd 1: Ch2, sc3 into 2nd ch from hook. Fsc11, fhdc1, fdc10, fhdc1. Hdc5 into ch at base of last st. (This creates a fan of 6 hdc at what will become the toe of the slipper.) Turn. Working along opposite edge of foundation: dc10, hdc1, sc11, 3sc in initial ch space. (This creates a fan of 6 sc at what will become the heel.) 56 sts. Join with sl st in first sc.

Rnd 2: Ch1. Hdc3 in same sc as sl st, hdc to 6 toe stitches. In the 5 spaces between these stitches, work: dc2, dc1, dc3, dc1, dc2. (9 stitches over the toe.) Hdc down other side to heel, hdc3 in last st. Join with sl st in first hdc. 65 sts.

Rnd 3: Ch1. Hdc in same hdc as sl st, hdc to the 3 middle stitches of the toe. Work dc2, dc1, dc2 over these sts. Hdc to heel. Join with sl st in first hdc. 67 sts.

Rnd 4: Repeat Row 3, except working the toe stitches as hdc2, hdc1 (pm), hdc2. 69 sts.

Rnd 5: Ch1. Hdc blo in same hdc as sl st, hdc blo around, moving marker up as you come to it. Join with sl st in first hdc.

Rnd 6: Ch1. Hdc in same hdc as sl st, hdc around, moving marker up as you come to it. Join with sl st in first hdc.

Rnd 7: Ch1. Hdc in same hdc as sl st, hdc to 8 stitches before marker (counting st the marker is in as the eighth st). Hdc2tog 4 times. Move marker up. Hdc2tog 4 times. Hdc to heel. Join with sl st in first hdc. 61 sts.

Rnd 8: Ch4.in next hdc and foll 2 hdc, hdc to 4 stitches before marker (counting st the marker is in as the fourth st). Dc4, move marker up, dc4. Hdc to 4 stitches before end of round. Dc4. Join with sl st in top of ch4.

Rnd 9: Ch1. Hdc in same st as sl st, hdc to 2 stitches before marker (counting st the marker is in as the second st). Dc2tog, remove marker, dc2tog 2 times. Hdc to heel. Join with sl st in first hdc. 58 sts.

Rnd 10: Ch1. *Hdc, ch1, skip next st; repeat from * around. Join with sl st in first hdc.

Rnd 11: Ch1. Rsc in each ch1 sp around. Join with sl st in first rsc. Break yarn, tie off.

Weave in ends. Blocking not needed, your foot does the work.

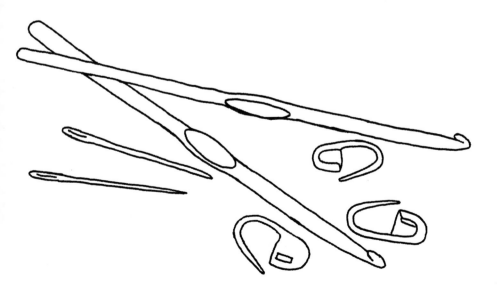

Isolde

TRISTAN AND ISOLDE
Folk Tale

THE LEGEND OF SLEEPY HOLLOW
Washington Irving

Stirring the pot — I knit in much the same way as I cook: a bit of this and a pinch of that with a substitution here and the odd addition there. I never get the exact same thing twice, but I can get close enough if I try. I think knitting should be the same.

The first sweater I ever knit was supposed to be a cowl-neck tunic. It was the only sweater pattern I owned. I had been knitting for about 6 months and had produced a long series of scarves using as few purl stitches as possible because I thought they were hard to do. As I was getting ready to knit this pattern my daughter asked if I would knit her a sweater before she left for university (in 3 weeks). In a fit of maternal *panic/love* I said yes — sure that any sweater I knit her would keep her safe from all harm and cold. But, she said, she didn't really like tunics so could I make it shorter? Yes. And more fitted? Sure. And maybe not a cowl neck? Okay. Could it be a V−neck? No problem. And the sleeves? Well, she wanted different ones. So, I started knitting along and, using the pattern as a very rough guide, I set out to create what she wanted without ever once considering that I clearly lacked any experience in what I was doing.

It turned out great, even though the handspun yarn I used made it too warm to wear except in the dead of winter. She loved it anyway.

I knit things I see in pictures. I knit by winging it. I knit what I know will work for me. My sock patterns typically have the same heel and toe because those are the heel and toe that fit my foot. If you have found a different type that fits your foot better, then by all means, use the one that fit you. If you need a deeper heel, then lengthen the heel and pick up a few more gusset stitches to compensate. Improvise to your heart's content, but never be afraid of your knitting.

Isolde was like that, afraid to love but knowing she would love Tristan with all her heart till the day they died. Knowing she was trapped by the potion and yet doing her best as bravely as she could. She defied convention and the morals of the time because she had no choice. The choice was taken away from her and she did the best with what she could control, as did Tristan. They were bold because they had to be in order to salvage what happiness they could. All of us, to a greater or lesser degree, will find ourselves someday reaching deep inside us to summon strength like theirs.

Initially I didn't want to list a gauge in the pattern because I knit tighter than the average knitter. I used to knit like I was knitting lifeboats for the HMS Titanic. However, I have learned to relax and loosen up — a bit. But that is a relative statement. I still knit tight. We are all individuals and it's as ridiculous to say "you have to knit to this gauge" as it is to say to someone who is clearly making fabric, "you're knitting wrong. You must knit like me." Regardless of the fear, please play with your knitting. Be adventurous and try new ways to make it how you would like it to be. Go up a needle size if the item seems to be a bit small. Add a pattern repeat if you think you need to. Try a new technique. We've included lots of resources for you. Be brave.

Oh. And have fun.

And don't worry about failure. It's not world peace we are working on here. My failures tend to be apocalyptic since I never have the good sense to stop when I see that all is going horribly awry. Oh no, I just keep knitting and improvising and changing things in the wild and doomed hope that it will suddenly be "ok". It happens — to some of us more than others. The key is to let go and move on.

And laugh.

I hope you will take these patterns and play with them, change them up a bit and make them your own. Own them, as my kids would say. And stir the pot a bit. Just to keep things fresh.

— Meg

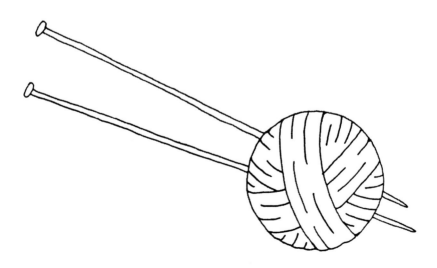

ISOLDE
Designed by Meg Warren

I wanted these socks to reflect Isolde's role both at home in Ireland and at her new home in Cornwall when she marries King Mark. I wanted to create a pattern that was refined and reflective of her role as a Queen.

SIZE
One size fits most women

FINISHED MEASUREMENTS
Foot circumference 8in [20.5cm]

Egalité

MATERIALS
- [MC] The March Hare sock yarn [75% superwash wool, 25% nylon; 455yd/416m per 100g skein; 18 WPI], color: Isolde; 1 skein for calf length and 2 skeins for knee length – any true fingering weight yarn can be substituted.
- Set of four US 2 [2.75mm] double pointed needles
- Set of four US 1 [2.25mm] double pointed needles

GAUGE
36 sts and 50 rows = 4in [10cm] in stockinette with smaller needles

PATTERN BEGINS
Cuff
Cast on 72 stitches using the larger needles and divide onto 3 needles to join in the round being careful not to twist the stitches. Work Rnds 1-28 of Chart A (page 37).

Leg
Change to smaller needles. Work Rnd 29 of Chart A, then work following Chart B (page 38) to desired length. Make a note of which rnd you stopped on.

Heel Flap
To begin the heel flap, k33, k2tog all onto one needle. Arrange the rem 37 stitches evenly over the other two needles. The 35 stitches on needle 1 will be your heel stitches and those holding on needles 2-3 will be your instep stitches.

For the flap:
Row 1 [WS]: Sl1 kwise wyif, purl to end.
Row 2 [RS]: Sl1 kwise wyif, *k1, sl1 kwise wyif; rep from * to end.
Rep these two rows 16 times (32 rows) or until the heel flap measures 2.25in [5.5cm], ending with a RS row.

Heel Turn
Row 1 [WS]: Sl1, p18, p2tog, p1, turn.
Row 2 [RS]: Sl1, k4, ssk, k1, turn.
Row 3: Sl1, purl to 1 stitch before the gap made by turning, p2tog, p1, turn.
Row 4: Sl1, knit to 1 stitch before the gap, k2tog, k1, turn.
Rep Rows 3-4 until all of the sts have been worked, ending with a RS row. 20 sts rem.

Gusset
Rnd 1 [RS]: With the same needle that holds the heel sts, pick up and knit 16 sts along the left side of the heel flap. With a second needle, work across instep sts keeping continuity of Chart B pattern. With a third needle, pick up and knit 16 sts along the right side of the heel flap, then knit 10 of the heel sts off of first needle. This point is the beg of the rnd from now on.
Rnd 2: Knit to the last 3 sts on needle 1, k2tog, k1. Work in established pattern over needle 2. On needle 3, k1, ssk, k to end.
Rnd 3: Knit all sts on needle 1, work in pattern over needle 2, knit all sts on needle 3.
Repeat Rows 2-3 until needles 1 and 3 each have 17 sts. 71 sts in total.

Foot
Continue working in pattern over instep sts and stockinette over sole sts until foot measures desired length less 2.25in [5.5cm] for toe shaping.

Optional: If desired foot length and continuity of pattern permit, after completing a Rnd 12 of Chart B you may switch to Chart C (page 39) to create pointed toe detail. In order that toe decreases should not interfere with the pattern, you would need to begin Chart C at least 4 rnds before starting to shape the toe.

Otherwise, you may simply stop wherever you are in Chart B and switch to working all sts in stockinette when beginning the toe shaping.

Toe
Rnd 1: Needle 1: Knit to the last 3 sts, k2tog, k1. Needle 2: K1, ssk, knit or work Chart C to the last 3 sts, k2tog, k1. Needle 3: K1, ssk, knit to end.
Rnd 2: Knit all sts on needle 1, knit or work Chart C pattern on needle 2, knit all sts on needle 3.
Rep Rnds 1-2 until 23 sts rem.
Next rnd: Needle 1: Knit to the last 3 sts, k2tog, k1. Needle 2: K1, ssk, knit or work Chart C to the last 3 sts, k3tog, k1. Needle 3: K1, ssk, knit to end.
Knit needle 1 stitches onto needle 3 and graft toe closed.

Chart A

24	23	22	21	20	19	18	17	16	15	14	13	12	11	10	9	8	7	6	5	4	3	2	1	Row
●	●	●	●	●	●	●	●	●	●	●	●	●	●	●	●	●	●	●	●	●	●	●	●	29
																								28
●	●	●	●	●	●	●	●	●	●	●	●	●	●	●	●	●	●	●	●	●	●	●	●	27
●		●			●			●			●			●			●			●				26
	●		●			●			●			●			●			●			●			25
	●			●			●			●			●			●			●				●	24
●		●			●			●			●			●			●			●				23
	●			●			●			●			●			●			●				●	22
		●		●				●		●			●		●				●		●			21
●		●			●			●			●			●			●			●				20
●	●	●	●	●	●	●	●	●	●	●	●	●	●	●	●	●	●	●	●	●	●	●	●	19
																								18
●	●	●	●	●	●	●	●	●	●	●	●	●	●	●	●	●	●	●	●	●	●	●	●	17
																								16
			●	●	●	●			●	●	●	●					●	●	●	●				15
		●	●	●	●				●	●	●	●				●	●	●	●					14
	●	●	●	●				●	●	●	●				●	●	●	●						13
●	●	●	●				●	●	●	●				●	●	●	●							12
●	●	●				●	●	●	●				●	●	●	●							●	11
●	●	●	●					●	●	●	●				●	●	●	●						10
	●	●	●	●				●	●	●	●				●	●	●	●						9
		●	●	●	●				●	●	●	●				●	●	●	●					8
			●	●	●	●				●	●	●	●				●	●	●	●				7
●	●	●	●	●	●	●	●	●	●	●	●	●	●	●	●	●	●	●	●	●	●	●	●	6
																								5
●	●	●	●	●	●	●	●	●	●	●	●	●	●	●	●	●	●	●	●	●	●	●	●	4
●	●			●	●			●	●			●	●			●	●			●	●			3
●	●			●	●			●	●			●	●			●	●			●	●			2
																								1

CHART B

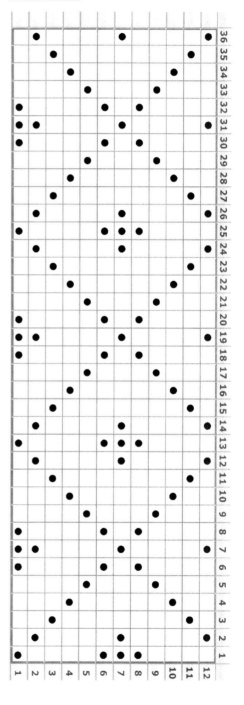

CHART C

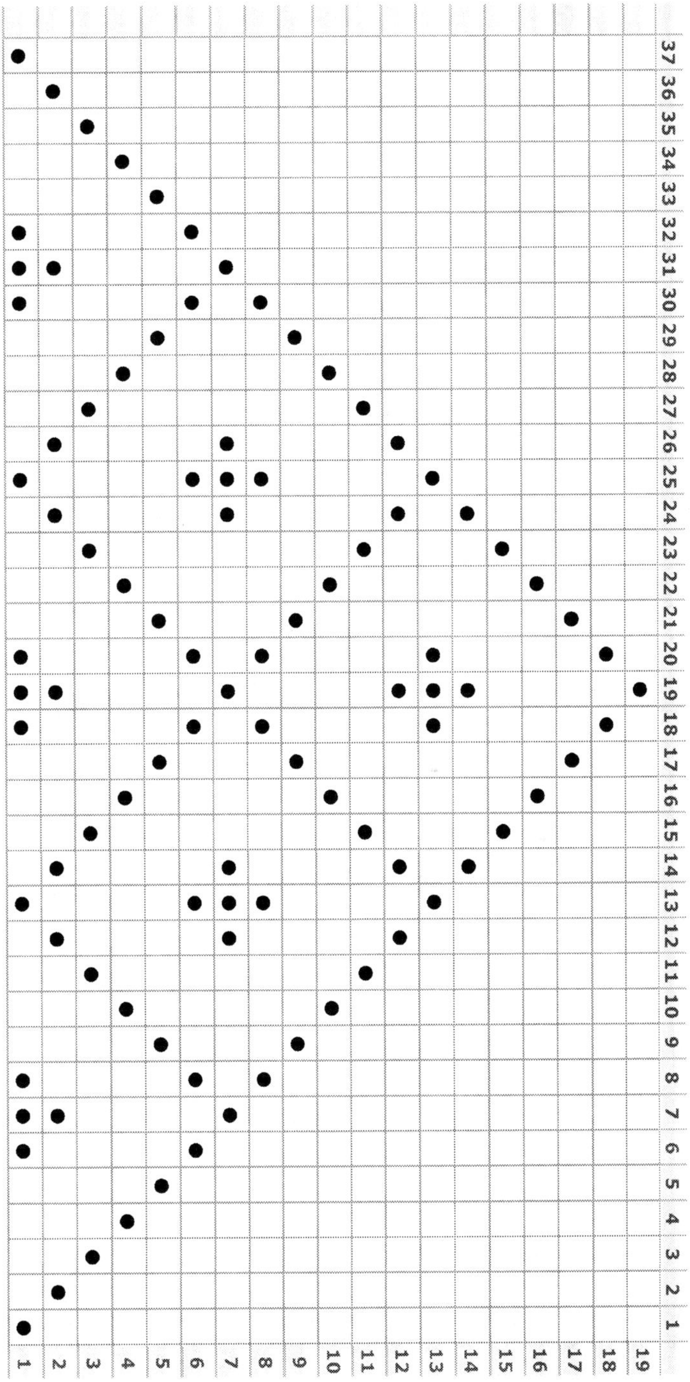

TRISTAN
Designed by Meg Warren

I loved the idea of a sock pattern that would reflect the rocks and the castles of stone in Cornwall so I used a yarn that is as close as I could come to the cold gray stone that is found there and a pattern that somewhat resembles the cobblestone walls that are still present today.

SIZE
One size

Liber*té*

FINISHED MEASUREMENTS
Foot circumference 8.5in [21.5cm]

MATERIALS
➤ The March Hare sock yarn [75% superwash wool and 25% nylon; 455yd/416m per 100g skein; 18 WPI], 1 skein color Tristan – any true fingering weight yarn can be substituted.
➤ Set of four US 1 [2.25mm] double pointed needles

GAUGE
36 sts and 50 rows = 4in [10cm] in stockinette

STITCH GUIDE
Box Stitch (multiple of 4 sts)
Rnds 1-2: *K2, p2; rep from * to end.
Rnds 3-4: *P2, k2; rep from * to end.
Rep Rnds 1-4.

4	3	2	1	
		●	●	4
		●	●	3
●	●			2
●	●			1

PATTERN BEGINS
Cast on 72 stitches and divide over 3 needles. Join to work in the round, being careful not to twist.

Cuff
Rnd 1: *K4, p4; rep from * to end.
Rep Rnd 1 for 1.5in [4cm]

Leg
Work in Box Stitch for desired length.

Heel Flap
To begin the heel flap, k32 sts onto one needle. Arrange the remaining stitches evenly over the other two needles. The 32 sts on needle 1 will be your heel stitches and the 40 sts holding on needles 2-3 will be your instep stitches.

For the flap:
Row 1 [WS]: Sl1 kwise wyif, purl to end.
Row 2 [RS]: Sl1 kwise wyif, *k1, sl1 kwise wyif; rep from * to end.
Repeat these two rows 18 times (36 rows) until the heel flap measures 2.5in [6.5cm], ending with a RS row.

Heel Turn
Row 1 [WS]: Sl1, p16, p2tog, p1, turn.
Row 2 [RS]: Sl1, k3, ssk, k1, turn.
Row 3: Sl1, purl to 1 stitch before the gap made by turning, p2tog, p1, turn.
Row 4: Sl1, knit to 1 stitch before the gap, k2tog, k1, turn.
Rep Rows 3-4 until all of the sts have been worked, ending with a RS row. 18 sts rem.

Gusset
Rnd 1 [RS]: With the same needle holding the heel sts, pick up and knit 18 sts along the left side of the heel flap. With a second needle, work across instep sts maintaining continuity of Box Stitch. With a third needle, pick up and knit 18 sts along the right side of the heel flap, then knit 9 of the heel sts off of first needle. This point is the beg of the rnd from now on.
Rnd 2: Knit to the last 3 sts on needle 1, k2tog, k1. Work in est patt over needle 2. On needle 3, k1, ssk, k to end.
Rnd 3: Knit all sts on needle 1, work in pattern over needle 2, knit all sts on needle 3.
Repeat Rows 2-3 until needles 1 and 3 each have 18 sts.

Foot
Continue working in pattern over instep sts and stockinette over sole sts until foot measures desired length, less 2.5in [6.5cm] for toe. Knit 1 rnd over all three needles.

Toe
Rnd 1: Needle 1: Knit to the last 3 sts, k2tog, k1. Needle 2: K1, ssk, knit to last 3 sts, k2tog, k1. Needle 3: K1, ssk, knit to end.
Rnd 2: Knit all sts.
Rep Rnds 1-2 until 16 sts rem. Knit needle 1 stitches onto needle 3 and graft toe closed.

ON THE **WWMDFK?** WEBSITE:

Feeling the need for a real break? Try some Flaming Glühwein!

Van Tassel Mittens

VAN TASSEL MITTENS
Designed by Meg Warren

I designed these mittens for fun. I liked the idea of random snowflakes drifting through a dark and desolate wood, such as you find in "The Legend of Sleepy Hollow" by Washington Irving. Imagine barren trees and dry leaves underfoot and the first snowflakes of winter beginning to drift down.

SIZE
Women's Small

FINISHED MEASUREMENTS
Hand circumference 7in [18cm]

Materials
- [MC] The March Hare wool silk blend [70% merino wool and 30% silk; [435 yd/398m per 100g skein, 18 WPI], 1 skein color Victoria's Ballgown – any true fingering weight yarn can be substituted.
- [CC] The March Hare wool silk blend, 1 skein color Sterling
- Set of five US 1 [2.25mm] double pointed needles
- Waste yarn

GAUGE
36 sts and 50 rows = 4in [10cm] in stockinette. To make larger mittens, go up one or two needle sizes. A gauge of 32 sts to 4in [10cm] would make mittens 8in [20.5cm] around the hand.

STITCH GUIDE
Corrugated Rib (multiple of 4 sts)
Rnd 1: *K2 with MC, p2 with CC; rep from * to end.
Rep rnd 1.

PATTERN BEGINS
Cuff
Cast on 80 stitches and divide evenly over 4 needles. Join, being careful not to twist the stitches. Work 20 rnds garter stitch (knit and purl alternate rnds).

Work the 22 rnds of Chart A.
With MC, k 1 rnd.
Next rnd: Knit, dec 4 sts evenly spaced. 76 sts.
K 1 rnd.
Next rnd: Knit, dec 6 sts evenly spaced. 70 sts.
Rep the last 2 rnds once more. 64 sts rem.
Work 5 rnds corrugated rib.
With MC, k 2 rnds.

Redistribute the sts so you have 38 sts split between needles 1 and 2 for the back of the hand, and 26 sts split between needles 3 and 4 for the palm.

Knit following charts B and C through Rnd 18.

Left Mitten: On Rnd 19, prepare sts for the thumb as follows: Work following charts to st 22 on palm; using waste yarn, knit sts 22 through 36; cut waste yarn. Slip the waste yarn sts back to the left-hand needle and knit them again in pattern using MC and CC. Work to end of rnd.

Right Mitten: On Rnd 19, prepare sts for the thumb as follows: Work following charts to st 3 on palm; using waste yarn, knit sts 3 through 20; cut waste yarn. Slip the waste yarn sts back to the left-hand needle and knit them again in pattern using MC and CC. Work to end of rnd.

Continue following charts as set through the end.

When you have reached the top of the mitten, break yarn, thread the tail on a darning needle, run through the rem sts and pull closed.

To knit the thumb, carefully remove the waste yarn and slide the 15 top and 15 bottom stitches onto 2 needles. To avoid a hole along the side of the thumb pick up an additional stitch on each side and k2tog when knitting around the first time.

Work following Chart D. The right half of the chart shows the "outside" of the thumb and the left half the "inside" (the side that faces the palm).
When you have reached the top of the thumb, break yarn and finish off as for the top of the mitten.

FINISHING
Weave in your ends and then wash and block.

ON THE **WWMDFK?** WEBSITE:

Nothing says "Autumn in New England" like a big pumpkin. And nothing says, "I'm the best cook you'll ever meet" like hot, spiced pumpkin soup served in a pumpkin tureen.

Should you wish to add tassels, I have attached them to the outer edge of the wrist where they are pretty but out of the way. See page 130 for basic tassel instructions that can be applied to any project, or page 197 for visual instructions.

Chart A

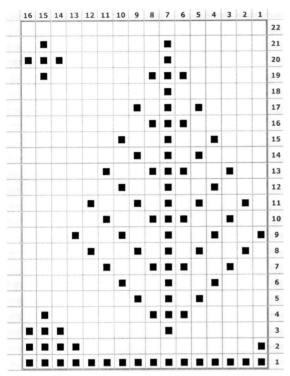

Chart D (l: inside of thumb, r: outside of thumb)

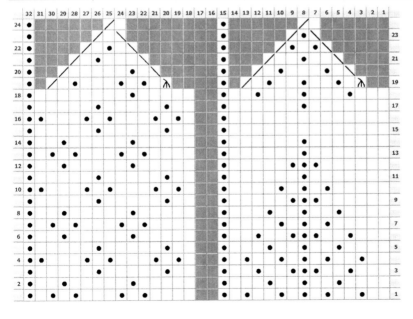

Chart B (back of left hand)

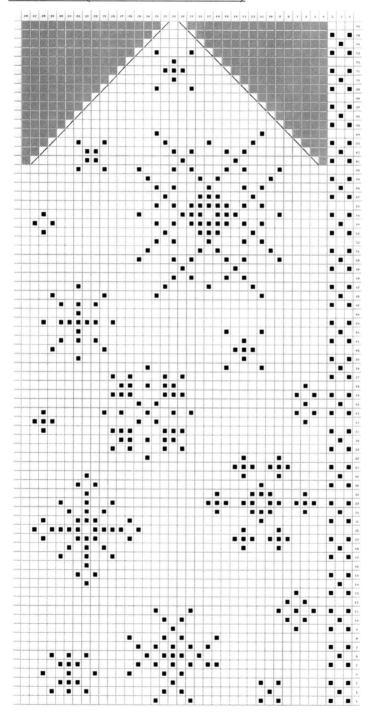

CHART C (LEFT PALM)

CHART B (BACK OF RIGHT HAND)

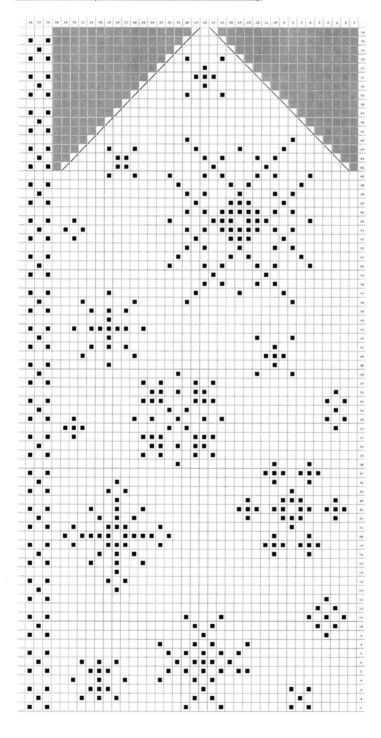

CHART C (RIGHT PALM)

The Mermaid's Lagoon

INTERLUDE I
Peter Pan — J.M. Barrie

Even though most of us think of it as *Peter Pan*, the play was originally titled *Peter and Wendy*. This small change carries a lot of weight with me. The iconic Peter who never grows up and never changes is not really the center of the story. The real protagonist is our quiet little Wendy.

Before Peter ever arrives, she is already starting to explore the balance between the creativity and freedom of childhood and the world of responsibility that adulthood is bringing closer to her every day. Throughout the story, we see Wendy as the mother, the caretaker, the mender, and the peacemaker. While the boys play at adventures, Wendy's imaginings include marriage, and children, and caring for a home. Wendy does not lack interest in the wild and fantastic surroundings of the Never Land. Wendy would love to swim with the mermaids, if they would only let her. But Wendy knows that after the adventures, you still need to take care of the holes in your (or, rather, the boy's) pants' knees.

This balance is central to the story. Peter never learns to face responsibility. The stumbles and disappointments in Peter's life are soon forgotten and may as well have never happened. Everything is a first time for Peter and he never learns or changes. Wendy's parents, on the other end of the spectrum, are caught up in work and responsibility. Her father is focused on how things should and ought to be — the appearance of things. It takes losing his children to that fanciful world of possibility for him to stop worrying about how he is seen by society and bring the whimsy of play back into his world. Wendy is in that magical time between these extremes and has the chance to find a place for each in her life.

We live in a world today where adults are often looked at askance when they play at adventures and imagine the possibilities around them. We have hard-line divisions between the work of adults and the play of children. Creativity is something we are expected to grow out of. Not that long ago, before the ubiquitous presence of televisions, even adults had to make their own entertainment. Puppet theaters were common in many homes. Printed characters and scenery that could be cut out and hand colored were sold as Penny Sheets with matching scripts. They were one of the small ways that play was present in the lives of even the most efficient and responsible adults. I hope these shadow puppets will help bring some of that play into your lives as well.

—Jen

N.B., as fiber artists, it is fascinating to see how often Wendy is working on some kind of stitching… at one point, she is even seen turning a heel!

THE MERMAID'S LAGOON
Designed by Jen Minnis

Everyone is familiar with making shadows dance on the walls, trying to make different shapes come to life. As Terry Pratchett would say, "Do deformed rabbit, it's my favorite!" The same principles that we used when we played with light as children are what will make these puppets come alive now — a light, something to block the light, and a screen for the shadow to fall on. It's that simple.

There are many options for a screen. Anything that the light will pass through will work, but the simplest is an old sheet tacked up in an open doorway. The audience sits on one side of the screen with the lights turned off. On the other side of the screen, the puppeteers act out the scenes by holding the puppets between the screen and a bright light behind the puppets. The resulting shadow is cast on the screen and visible to the audience. The audience never sees the actual puppets — only their shadows.

Other options for screens are tent walls, a large frame mounted with a sheet of paper, or a cardboard box with one side cut out and covered with thin paper. Any handy light source can be used, but the brighter the better. Fluorescent lights, sadly, don't seem to give good crisp shadows. Experiment with your set up to find your favorite stage and lighting.

MATERIALS
- Black poster board, black cardstock, or cereal box material
- Freezer paper cut into letter sized sheets
- fine tipped craft knife
- Self healing cutting mat
- Bamboo skewers
- White glue (Elmer's or Tacky Glue type)
- 18 gauge wire (copper or brass work well)
- Old white sheet

The first thing to think about when making shadow puppets is your choice of material. Dark or black material will naturally block the light better than lighter colored material. But any material that is thick enough will cast a shadow. If you don't have any dark material and your puppets aren't casting enough of a shadow, try coloring them with markers or paint. The thicker the material you choose, the sturdier your puppets will be. However, the same rule applies to how difficult it will be to cut out.

If you will be playing with your puppets with young children, then choose a thicker material and eliminate the smaller details of the patterns to make them easier to cut. Optionally, you can also laminate your puppets to help make them sturdier. Trim the lamination close to the edges of the puppets. The clear lamination will allow the light to pass through and the details of the cut puppet will still cast a good shadow. Laminated puppets are less aesthetically pleasing when displayed between performances, but for puppets that will see heavy use, they have a much-improved lifespan.

Once you have chosen your materials, it is time to start making your puppets. Freezer paper is a wonderful crafting tool. When heated, the plastic side of the freezer paper will gently melt, allowing it to temporarily bond with materials like paper or fabric. Most inkjet printers should have no problem printing onto freezer paper. Laser printers, on the other hand, use heat as part of the printing process and don't play nice with freezer paper. Print or copy the patterns onto the paper side of your sheets of freezer paper. Feel free to scale the puppets up to make them easier to cut, just be sure to scale proportionally.

> **ON THE WWMDFK? WEBSITE:**
>
> Download a file which contains all the images needed for creating your own Mermaid's Lagoon set.

With the plastic side of the freezer paper toward your cardstock or poster board, iron them on a wool/silk setting, bonding the freezer paper to the puppet material. Do not overheat it. Just iron until the freezer paper is fully stuck down. If you heat it too much, the freezer paper will not peel away easily later. (Trust me! I've learned the hard way!)

Now, to cut! Using your craft knife, on a protected surface such as a sheet of glass or a self-healing cutting mat, cut through the freezer paper and puppet material following the pattern outlines. Start with the smaller areas and the more detailed cuts. When you have the option, work from the center out. The longer you leave the outer edges attached to the larger sheet, the more stable your piece will be while cutting. Take your time. Don't expect to cut out all the puppets in an afternoon. The more time you take to cut carefully, the better your puppets will be in the end. Straight cuts are easier than curves. Even though they look complex, the jagged areas of the crocodile's teeth and back are some of the easiest to do. Try to cut away from corners, when possible. Stab your knifepoint into the corner to start the cut and draw out along the pattern line. For curves, try turning the material you are cutting, not the knife. For very tight curves, use just the tip of the knife and make small stab cuts around the curve. Our minds smooth these edges out more than you think when you look at the whole pattern and not just the close detail. If you're not comfortable with a craft knife, sharp small-bladed embroidery scissors are a possible substitution.

Now that you have a puppet cut out, you can peel the freezer paper pattern away. As a wonderful bonus, you now also have a reusable stencil! You can iron the freezer paper shape onto paper or fabric several more times before it loses its ability to stick. Try ironing it onto paper and using a makeup sponge to pounce rubber-stamping ink around the edges. Or iron it onto an old t-shirt and use fabric paint to decorate. Try grouping several shapes together to create a scene. If you were careful with your cutting, you might even have both positive and negative stencils to play with. Experiment and have fun!

Ok, now back to the puppets!

You have your character shape… but how do you hold it? It is time to make some control rods. Simple rods can be glued right onto the puppets, but they require you to hold your puppet straight up and down close to your screen. Hinged rods allow you to hold them at an angle, and it helps hide the shadow of the rods. Cut some of your puppet material into 1/4" strips. Cut these into 1" sections. Fold these sections in half. These are your hinges. They will allow you to glue your rods on at an angle. Glue your bamboo skewer or dowel to the inside of one side of a hinge.

> *If you are using bamboo skewers, glue the pointed end into the hinge and prevent it from becoming a lethal puppet weapon.*

Once the glue has dried, you can glue the other side of the hinge to the back of a puppet. A cup or vase filled with rice makes a great holder for drying puppets or display tool for puppets not in use.

A few of the puppets in this theater set need special details formed out of wire. The wire allows you to make thin shadow lines without having them bend and tear at the first touch. The shadow cast will look the same no matter what material you use to make it. Form a hook for the Captain and a tail for the kite from the wire and glue them onto the backs of the puppets. Photos of this process are available on the WWMDfK? website.

You can use additional sections of wire or pieces of bamboo skewer as supports glued to the back of thin or fragile parts your puppets. Be careful, however, about how much weight you add to your puppets. If they become top heavy and won't hang straight you can use a bit of wire glued to the lower section of the puppet as an invisible weight to balance them out.

Color can be added to areas of your puppets, if you wish, by filling cut out areas with colored tissue paper. Try adding some yellow to Starkey's lantern or some rainbow colors to the mermaids' tails. Now that you have your puppets, let's talk scenery.

The simplest method is to just pin your scenery pieces directly onto your screen. This works very well for most shadow puppet plays, but for our lagoon scene, we need something a bit more dynamic. You see, our scenery is not just static, it changes: The pirates' dinghy is brought into the scene — and the tide rises — so we need to be able to make changes mid–action.

Because your screen/stage area will vary in size, I have not made a specific length for the waves. Instead, cut out the section of waves and use it as a template to trace a wave pattern long enough to fill your available area. I used cardstock to cut most of my puppets, but when it came time to cut out the scenery, I switched to poster board to get large enough pieces. I needed three long sections of waves to fill my stage area and make the water rise on Tiger Lily.

The two shores, Marooner's Rock, and the pirate's dingy are all cut in the same way you cut out the puppets. If you choose to pin them onto the sheet, than you are all set. However, in order to make them changeable, you will need some bases: two of each type of the scenery bases. Cut on the solid lines to form slits and fold on the dashed lines: the small strip bases are for the rock and the dingy. Accordion-fold these bases and slip the pieces into the slits to make them stand independently. On the two shore pieces, measure along the bottom edge from the outside corner and cut a slit 1/2" tall at the 1/2" and 1-1/2" marks. Do this to each end of all three waves as well. These slits will fit into the slits on the larger bases. The lowest position on the bases will be for your first section of waves. The second set of slits is for the shores. This is the basic scene setup. Set these on a table behind your screen and you are all set to act out the first part of the lagoon scene. As the scene progresses and the tide rises, you will add your additional wave sections to the bases, obscuring more and more of the rock beneath the water: first when the pirates bring Tiger Lily... and again when Peter and Wendy are stranded alone.

Now you are all set to play!

With the patterns provided, you will be able to play out the Mermaid's Lagoon scene of Peter and Wendy. Why not snag the audio from Librivox.org to play while you act it out!? Think about making some more puppets of your own to fill out the rest of the play, or to adventure into other stories. Take a look at photos or images you see in magazines and advertisements. Are there any poses you think would make good shadows? Inspiration is waiting everywhere around you!

And a final note — when the play was originally published and shown on stage, Tinkerbell was "acted" by a light instead of an actor. Although Tink isn't in this scene, you can still include her in your puppet set: just grab an inexpensive laser pointer at an office supply store and bring her to life!

Here are just a few of the delightful images for this playset that you'll find on the WWMDfK? website.

Bertha's Mad, Mysterious Möbius

JANE EYRE
Currer Bell (Charlotte Brontë)

Bertha Mason…
Rochester's Creole wife…
The madwoman in the attic…

Literary critics through the years have written pages and pages about her. As a freshman in college, I took a course on women's literature wherein we read not only *Jane Eyre*, but also *Wide Sargasso Sea*, by Jean Rhys. I was so taken with this story that the novel is one of only a handful of college books I still own. *Wide Sargasso Sea* is not exactly "the story of Jane Eyre from the madwoman's perspective," but more the story of Bertha/Antoinette, which happens to overlap Jane's story at points. It covers some of Antoinette's childhood, her marriage to Rochester, her descent into madness and, finally, her death as recounted by Grace Poole. *Wide Sargasso Sea* is a fascinating novel, which I highly recommend you read right after reading *Jane Eyre*, while Jane's story is still fresh in your mind.

Bertha/Antoinette is a vivid contrast to Jane:

> ᔥ— Exotic and beautiful — not staid and plain
> ᔥ— Wild and sensual — not controlled and chaste
> ᔥ— Allowing her emotions to drive her — not subordinating them to her morals
> ᔥ— Superstitious instead of faithful
> ᔥ— Headstrong, allowing her imagination and fancy free rein — not keeping them suppressed, letting them out only from time to time in her artwork
> ᔥ— Openly enjoying sex instead of resisting its allure
> ᔥ— Sinful and "bad" — not holy and "good"

As shawls are fixtures during transitions for Jane Eyre, "the madwoman in the attic" has become a fixture in literature. Having something hidden in the attic is now a recognized literary device signifying secrets and madness. As much as Jane Eyre has influenced young women's idealized expectations of romance and love, the book has also affected literature in general.

As I read *Wide Sargasso Sea* again, I was struck by the lushness of the island environment as described by Antoinette. I was also fascinated by the recurring appearance of birds. As one would expect from Bertha's role in *Jane Eyre*, candles and fire are important to the story. Overall, I came away with a very extravagant, sensual image of Antoinette, and I wanted her scarf to have a similar feel.

Recently, I have been fascinated by the Möbius construction as described in Cat Bordhi's books, and the mysterious twistiness, the "no right and wrong side" nature of it, seemed *à propos* for representing a madwoman. The single skein of Malabrigo Sock I had been saving in my stash "for something special" was clearly the perfect yarn for this project, and all the more so because it was Ravelry Red — about as un–Janeian a color as I could imagine. With thanks to Cat Bordhi for the inspiration, I give you Bertha's Mad, Mysterious Möbius. Though it may look complicated, the knitting is actually fairly straightforward once you get going. I promise. I'm not crazy.

— Erica

BERTHA'S MAD, MYSTERIOUS MÖBIUS
Designed by Erica Hernandez

Part of the mystery of Möbius construction is that it is neither bottom–up nor top–down, but more like "cast–on–out". The cowl begins with an orderly central "spine" of a cast–on from which emanate the sensual flames which later dissolve into an almost completely open fabric with little weight. Wear it wide over your shoulders, hanging straight down in a big "U", up over your head as a hood, doubled around your neck, or in some other way I haven't thought of. You may not be mad, but when you tell admirers that you knit it, everyone will think you have "mad skills."

Egalité

FINISHED MEASUREMENTS
Approx. 12in [30.5cm] tall x 35in [89cm] circumference

MATERIALS
- Malabrigo Yarns Sock [100% merino wool; 440 yards/110 grams per skein; 19 WPI], 1 skein Ravelry Red
- US 6 [4mm] circular needle, 47in [120cm] long
- Stitch marker

GAUGE
32 sts = 4in [10cm] over flame chevron pattern

PATTERN NOTES
For instructions on how to do the Möbius cast-on, please see *A Treasury of Magical Knitting* and *A Second Treasury of Magical Knitting* by Cat Bordhi. As of this writing, you can also find a wonderfully clear instructional video entitled "Intro to Möbius Knitting" posted by Cat herself on YouTube.

Have you knit a full round yet? Remember while knitting that you have completed one full round when your beg-of-rnd marker appears in the normal "beginning of round" place between your two needles, NOT when it is below your two needles. This makes more sense when you think of your cast-on round as a central spine from which you are knitting outward.

Note on rounds 4 & 5: Yes, the stitch count increases just during Rnd 4. The double yo is charted in one square as if were a single stitch because on Rnd 5, you purl into the first yo and drop the second one, indicated by a star on the chart, bringing the stitch count back to the original number.

SECTION ONE – FLAME CHEVRON

Flames – hot, sinuous, and sensual, they are fascinating, even mesmerizing. Flames can keep you warm or scar you forever, giving you either life or death. There are many stitch patterns with "flame" or "candle" in the name, but to my eyes, they more closely resembled leaves than flames. Flame chevron, however, really did conjure up for me the idea of flames climbing a wall or, perhaps, a bedside curtain.

Using Möbius method, cast on 189 stitches. Pm and knit 1 rnd plain (this is Rnd 1), then work the 48 rnds of Chart A. Note that only even-numbered rnds are shown on this chart; knit all odd-numbered rnds plain. Take care on rnds ending with a yo to keep the yo on the correct side of your stitch marker.

SECTION TWO – DISSOLVING LACE

As Bertha's sanity and reason dissolve, so does the cowl, melting into an increasingly open, flimsy lace pattern.

Work the 12 rnds of Chart B. Both odd- and even-numbered rounds are shown on this chart. Again, take care to keep yos that fall at the end of the rnd on the correct side of the marker.

FINISHING

Bind off using decreasing BO as foll: *K2tog. Slip the resulting st back to the left-hand needle. (If necessary, give the fabric a gentle tug to make sure your stitch isn't too tight.) Repeat from * until all sts are bound off.

Weave in ends, then wash and give a quick trip through the spin cycle to get out the excess water. Cat's favorite way of blocking a Möbius is to hang it off the end of an ironing board with the twist at the bottom.

OPTIONS

This cowl has a totally different look in different yarn. My first draft was in Louet Gems in Shamrock, and it conjured up a decidedly different mood, simply because of the color. If you enjoy knitting with beads, add some beads in the open yos or just on the edging. If you want some bling, use a yarn with a few sequins. For a more obvious flame look, use a natural white yarn, then dye your scarf red, orange and yellow. Want to feel even more opulent and decadent? Use TWO skeins of yarn and knit each section with double the number of rounds!

CHART A

7	6	5	4	3	2	1	
O						╱	48
O						╱	46
O						╱	44
O					╱		42
O				╱			40
O			╱				38
					O	╲	36
				O		╲	34
			O			╲	32
		O				╲	30
	O					╲	28
O						╲	26
O						╱	24
O					╱		22
O				╱			20
O			╱				18
O		╱					16
O	╱						14
					O	╲	12
				O		╲	10
			O			╲	8
		O				╲	6
	O					╲	4
O						╲	2

CHART B

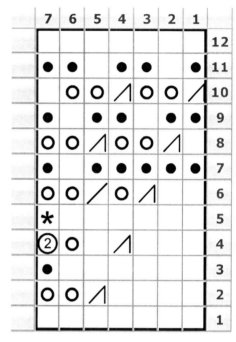

Note: in Chart B above, row 10/ column 1 is a k3tog (╱) and not a k2tog. The charting software's indicator for a pattern repeat is covering the edge of that stitch.

On the WWMDfK? website:

In honor of Bertha's place of origin, we would like to share a tropical drink worthy of her madness.

Hyde's Hooded Sweater

THE MYSTERIOUS CASE OF DR JEKYLL AND MR HYDE
Robert Louis Stevenson

"I had but to drink the cup, to doff at once the body of the noted professor, and to assume, like a thick cloak, that of Edward Hyde. I smiled at the notion."

Perhaps I have a different view of *The Strange Case of Dr. Jekyll and Mr. Hyde*. I have heard the argument that Dr. Jekyll was somehow trying to conquer the "bad" side of his self to become "good". That the motivation behind separating the proper side and the rough side of his personality was to somehow get rid of the rough side altogether. I just didn't get that. I don't see it. It's a stretch to think you could just get rid of the rotten side of your own egg. They're two parts of a whole. It's light and dark, man. Positive and negative, oil and vinegar — and I like that on my salad. It brings it all together. One can't really exist without the other (okay, maybe you can live without oil and vinegar, but really, that would make the world a pretty boring place).

"I saw that, of the two natures that contended in the field of my consciousness, even if I could rightly be said to be either, it was only because I was radically both."

Destroying either side seems like a losing proposition right off the bat to me. Our Doctor was a man of science, a man of logic, stuck in the Victorian era. The greatest power that era had over its people was the soul crushing morality, the overriding need to be proper. The class system would be a second massive societal force, in all its classist glory. These things I do see in the story — but are they the reason why Jekyll does what he does? He mentions morality a few times, but read further, or read the paragraph before, and Jekyll will make a claim that sends us back to science, to analytical thinking.

"...from an early date, even before the course of my scientific discoveries had begun to suggest the most naked possibility of such a miracle, I had learned to dwell with pleasure, as a beloved daydream, on the thought of the separation of these elements. If each, I told myself, could be housed in separate identities, life would be relieved of all that was unbearable; the unjust might go his way, delivered from the aspirations and remorse of his more upright twin; and the just could walk steadfastly and securely on his upward path, doing the good things in which he found his pleasure, and no longer exposed to disgrace and penitence by the hands of this extraneous evil."

I think the Doctor knew what he was going for. Not necessarily to destroy, to get rid of, but... to compartmentalize the portions of his psyche.

"I made my preparations with the most studious care. I took and furnished that house in Soho, to which Hyde was tracked by the police; and engaged as a housekeeper a creature

whom I knew well to be silent and unscrupulous. On the other side, I announced to my servants that a Mr. Hyde (whom I described) was to have full liberty and power about my house in the square; and to parry mishaps, I even called and made myself a familiar object, in my second character. I next drew up that will to which you so much objected; so that if anything befell me in the person of Dr. Jekyll, I could enter on that of Edward Hyde without pecuniary loss. And thus fortified, as I supposed, on every side, I began to profit by the strange immunities of my position."

Was he trying to make two polar sides of a person who could live two lives for themselves? He *was* building separate households and accounts and training the staff to treat him as two different people — which was easy because his personalities looked like the moral opposites they were. He even willed one side's belongings to the other. This was not a man who felt he was going to destroy the evil within himself. In a way, he was buying it a vacation house.

A man like that, he might not want to give up any part of either side of his "creation". Underneath, maybe he's a guy who wants all of it. He wants to have dinner with the other rich, upper-crust guys one night, and then go drinking and carousing with the lowlifes the other. That, to me, seems a more logical thought process. A slightly less morality-based pursuit and more of a pursuit of selfishness. Hey, I lived through the 80s and all that went with it, I get it. I get wanting to take that potentially embarrassing part of yourself and make it go elsewhere. I get not wanting be accountable for the party animal within.

"Men have before hired bravos to transact their crimes, while their own person and reputation sat under shelter. I was the first that ever did so for his pleasures. I was the first that could plod in the public eye with a load of genial respectability, and in a moment, like a schoolboy, strip off these lendings and spring headlong into the sea of liberty. But for me, in my impenetrable mantle, the safety was complete. Think of it – I did not even exist! Let me but escape into my laboratory door, give me but a second or two to mix and swallow the draught that I had always standing ready; and whatever he had done, Edward Hyde would pass away like the stain of breath upon a mirror; and there in his stead, quietly at home, trimming the midnight lamp in his study, a man who could afford to laugh at suspicion, would be Henry Jekyll."

But, we all know you can't have it all. Details of questionable activities would be hard to conceal, and it would take a lot of energy and effort covering up all the things along the line that connects the two parts of a person. It would be a full time job, plus overtime — that and, of course, the side effects, the *whoppers* of side effects. Just like being an addict, hiding this stuff would not be easy. Things start to get dicey on that front and that's where the idea for this sweater came along. In one part, it's proper — a little more formal than the average, with a long collar. On the other hand, the hood is right there, for when things start moving in a different direction and you feel more of a need to travel incognito. I guess I wanted to help the Doc out. Maybe it's being an enabler, but with this story, part of me wants to believe if he had more time, more control, he could have worked it out. Stevenson wrote a wacky timeline of a story. I have a hard time following it because it jumps from time to time and narrator to narrator. But I think I see a message in it. I like to think I do a good job rectifying the good and the bad within myself, and I do it within myself, because without both sides... I wouldn't be me.

— Gretchen

HYDE'S HOODED SWEATER
Designed by Gretchen Funk

When one needs to slip out of view, it is always good to have help. The proper attire is key. This jacket–like sweater for men or women (we can all have different sides) is meant to be stylish and flexible in any circumstance. The large collar can be pulled above the head and buttoned, to make a hood, and the pockets are integrally designed to conceal, well, whatever you may need to conceal.

SIZE
S (M, L, XL)

Liberté

FINISHED MEASUREMENTS
Chest 36 [40, 44, 48]in [91.5 (101.5, 112, 122)cm] (buttoned)
Length: 26 [27, 28, 29]in [66 (68.5, 71, 73.5)cm]

MATERIALS
- Briar Rose Fibers Abundance [100% wool; 750yd/686m per 456g skein; 9 WPI], 2 [2, 2, 3] skeins (please note: this yarn is dyed in one of a kind lots, and there is no color name)
- US 8 [5mm] circular needles, 32in (80cm) and 16in [40cm] long
- Set of four or five US 8 [5mm] double pointed needles
- 8 [8, 8, 9] 0.5in [15mm] buttons for hood
- Eight 0.75in [19mm] buttons for sweater. Buttons shown are by Jennie the Potter (*jenniethepotter.com*)
- Waste yarn
- US H [5mm] crochet hook
- Stitch markers, 6 in color A and 4 in color B

GAUGE
15 sts and 24 rows = 4in [10cm] in stockinette

STITCH GUIDE
Seed Stitch (even number of sts)
Row or rnd 1: *K1, p1; rep from * to end.
Row or rnd 2: *P1, k1; rep from * to end.
Rep Rows/Rnds 1-2.

PATTERN NOTES
Hoodie is knit seamlessly from the top down, beginning with the hood.

PATTERN BEGINS
Hood
With waste yarn, longer circular needle, and crochet provisional method (see Glossary, page 192), cast on 70 [72, 72, 78] sts.
Row 1 [WS]: Sl1 kwise, p1, [p1, k1] to last 2 sts, p2.
Row 2 [RS]: Sl1 kwise, k1, [k1, p1] to end.

Rep Rows 1-2 for 13in [33cm], ending with Row 1.

Yoke
Set-up row [RS]: Sl1 kwise, k1, pm color A, work 8 sts in est seed st patt, pm color A, k3 [3, 3, 4] (left front); pm color B, k9 [9, 9, 10] (left sleeve); pm color B, k3, pm color A, work 20 [22, 22, 24] sts in est seed st patt, pm color A, k3 (back); pm color B, k9 [9, 9, 10] (right sleeve); pm color B, k3 [3, 3, 4], pm color A, work 8 sts in est seed st patt, pm color A, k1, p1 (right front).

The A markers denote the panels of seed stitch; all sts outside the panels, with the exception of the 2-st selvage at each end of the row, are worked in stockinette. The B markers denote where you will make your raglan increases. Slip all markers as you come to them.

Neck and raglan shaping
Row 1 [WS]: Sl1 kwise, p1, work to last 2 sts keeping panels between A markers in seed st and working all other sts in stockinette, p2.

Row 2 [neck and raglan inc row]: Sl1 kwise, k1, work left front seed st panel, kfb, [work in est patts to 1 st before B marker, kfb, sl m, k1, kfb] four times, work to 1 st before right front seed st panel, kfb, work seed st panel, k1, p1. 10 sts inc'd.

Rep Rows 1-2 4 [6, 6, 6] times more. 120 [142, 142, 148] sts.

Raglan shaping
Row 1 [WS]: Sl1 kwise, p1, work in est patts to last 2 sts, p2.
Row 2 [RS]: Sl1 kwise, k1, work in est patts to last 2 sts, k1, p1.
Row 3: Rep Row 1.
Row 4 [raglan inc row]: Sl1 kwise, k1, [work in est patts to B marker, kfb, sl m, k1, kfb] four times, work in patt to last 2 sts, k1, p1. 8 sts inc'd.
Rep Rows 1-4 8 [8, 6, 5] times more. 192 [214, 198, 196] sts.

Rep Rows 3-4 only 4 [4, 8, 11] times. 224 [246, 262, 284] sts.

For sizes S and M, rep Row 3 once more and skip to Divide Body and Sleeves, below.

For sizes (L, XL) only:

Next row [WS]: Sl1 kwise, p1, work in est patts to last 2 sts, p2.
Next row [raglan inc row, body sections only]: Sl1 kwise, k1, [work in est patts to B marker, kfb, sl m, work to next B marker, sl m, kfb] twice, work to last 2 sts, k1, p1. 4 sts inc'd.
Rep these 2 rows [1, 2] times more, then work WS row only once. [270, 296] sts.

Divide Body and Sleeves
You should have in each section:
Back: 62 [68, 76, 84] sts
Each front: 36 [40, 44, 48] sts
Each sleeve: 45 [49, 53, 58] sts

Remove the B markers as you work the next row.
Next row [RS]: Sl1, k1, work in est patt to first B marker, sl all sts between first and second B markers to waste yarn, use backward loop method to cast on 4 sts, work in est patt to third B marker, sl all sts between third and fourth B markers to waste yarn, use backward loop method to cast on 4 sts, work in patt to last 2 sts, k1, p1. 142 [156, 172, 188] sts on needle.

Next row [WS]: Sl1 kwise, p1, work in est patts to last 2 sts, p2.

Lower Body
Work even, maintaining selvedges and seed st panels as established, until body measures 21 [22, 23, 24]in [53.5 (56, 58.5, 61)cm] from top of shoulder, ending with a WS row. AT THE SAME TIME, beg on first RS row, work a buttonhole on every 14th (14th, 16th, 16th) row as foll: Work to last 8 sts, k2tog, yo twice, p2tog, (k1, p1) twice. On the following row, work (k1, p1) into the double yo.

Pocket Opening
Next row [RS]: Work 18 [20, 20, 22] sts in patt. *With waste yarn, k16 [17, 18, 19]. Cut waste yarn. Slip the waste yarn sts back to the left-hand needle and knit them again with main yarn.* Work to last 34 [37, 38, 41] sts. Repeat from * to *. Work 18 [20, 20, 22] sts to end.

Hem
Work in seed st for 5in [12.5cm], maintaining selvedges and continuing to work buttonholes until there are 8 in total. Bind off loosely in pattern.

Sleeves
Place the 45 [49, 53, 58] held sts of sleeve on shorter circular needle.
Join yarn, pick up and knit 2 sts from underarm, pm for beg of rnd, pick up and knit 2 sts. Knit around sleeve to marker. 49 [53, 57, 62] sts.
Working in stockinette, dec 1 st on each side of marker on every 12th [11th, 10th, 8th] rnd

8 [9, 10, 12] times as foll: K2, ssk, k to last 4 sts, k2tog, k2. 33 [35, 37, 38] sts.
Work even until sleeve measures 17 [17, 17.5, 17.5]in [43 (43, 44.5, 44.5)cm] from underarm, or desired length less 1in [2.5cm].
Dec 1 [1, 1, 0] st at beg of next rnd. 32 [34, 36, 38] sts.
Work in seed st for 1in [2.5cm].
Bind off loosely in pattern.

Pockets
Carefully remove waste yarn. RS facing, place the 16 [17, 18, 19] sts from the top of the opening on one dpn, and the 16 [17, 18, 19] sts from the bottom on a second dpn. Join yarn, knit across first needle, pick up and k 1 st at corner of opening, knit across second needle, pick up and k 1 st at corner, pm for beg of rnd. 34 [36, 38, 40] sts.
Next rnd: [K16 (17, 18, 19), p1] twice.
Continue as set by last round for 3.5in [9cm].
Join the two sides using a three-needle bind off (see Glossary, page xx).

Top of Hood
Unzip provisional cast on from top of hood and place these 70 [72, 72, 78] sts on longer circular needle.

Applied I-cord with button loops:
(a video tutorial is available online)[1]
With WS facing, cast on 2 sts to left-hand needle.
*[K1, k2tog, slip these 2 sts back to left-hand needle] 4 times, k2, slip 2 sts back to left-hand needle; rep from * 7 [7, 7, 8] times more. 8 [8, 8, 9] button-loops formed. This should bring you approximately to the middle of the hood.
*K1, k2tog, slip these 2 sts back to left-hand needle; rep from * until hood sts are used up.
Bind off rem 2 sts.

FINISHING
Weave in ends. Wash and block. Attach buttons. Wear in good health, and good hiding.

ON THE WWMDFK? WEBSITE:

Feeling the need to bring your two sides back together? Maybe you need a nummy black and white cookie to tame your inner angst?

1 — http://www.youtube.com/watch?v=UJAzaa5bqZQ

SCHEMATIC

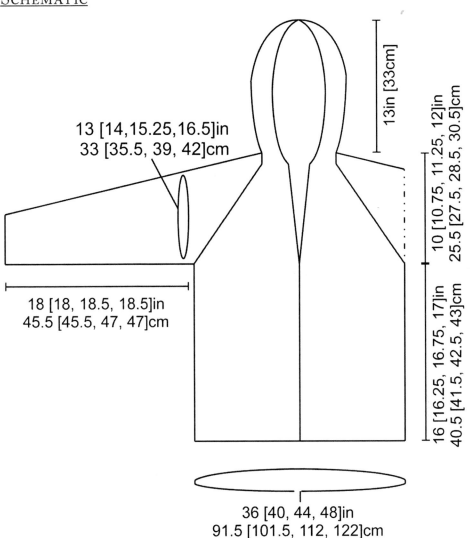

13in [33cm]

13 [14,15.25,16.5]in
33 [35.5, 39, 42]cm

10 [10.75, 11.25, 12]in
25.5 [27.5, 28.5, 30.5]cm

18 [18, 18.5, 18.5]in
45.5 [45.5, 47, 47]cm

16 [16.25, 16.75, 17]in
40.5 [41.5, 42.5, 43]cm

36 [40, 44, 48]in
91.5 [101.5, 112, 122]cm

FRANKENSTEIN
Mary Wollstonecraft Shelley

"Shall each man find a wife for his bosom, and each beast have his mate, and I be alone?"
— The Monster

Frankenstein's monster is one of literature's unsung heroes, as romantic and doomed as Bronte's Heathcliff. Unlike the shambling hulk popularized by Universal Studios in 1931, in Mary Shelley's novel the monster is intelligent, articulate, and seeking only to find his place in the world. Rejected by all — even his creator — as an abomination, the monster, in despair, turns to desperate means to force Victor Frankenstein into fashioning an equally monstrous companion, with whom he intends to run away into the wilds and live a vegetarian lifestyle. Victor (a brainless twit) does not come through, and all ends badly.

I can't help thinking that Match.com would have been a boon to the monster. He could have met a geeky vegan girl in an online chat, won her over with his intelligent discourse and enthusiasm for life; later confessed that he had "some appearance challenges" and then had a romantic rendezvous in a shadowy corner of Starbucks.

Re–reading Frankenstein while designing this pattern, I thought about how clothing is magnificent: while concealing the body, it can reveal the spirit within. Creating a mock–up of Universal Studio's variation of Frankenstein is my tongue-in-cheek way to reclaim the man from the monster.

This hood is for all of us who have felt like an outsider at one point or another, and who are looking for our monstrous kin with whom to share life's joys and sorrows.

P.S. It also lights up. Because eTextiles and Frankenstein were made for each other, of course.

— Syne

FRANKENHOOD
Designed by Syne Mitchell

This cozy Frankenstein-inspired hood features light-up neck bolts. A flat-top head and fringed bangs makes this excellent snow-boarding attire. For more mellow knitters, the illuminated neck bolts add both safety and fashion to twilight dog walks.

SIZE
Adult S/M (M/L)

Note: The only difference between the two sizes is the circumference of the collar piece. The hood should fit almost anyone.

FINISHED MEASUREMENTS
Head circumference: 20.5in (52.5cm)
Length: 13in (33cm)

Egalité

MATERIALS

- [MC] Cascade 220 [100% Peruvian Highland wool; 220yds/200m per 100g skein; 10 WPI]; 1 skein #1975 green
- [CC1] Cascade 220, 1 skein #1752 black
- [CC2] Grand Opera by Nashua Handknits [86% wool/9% viscose/5% metallized polyester; 128yds/117m per 50g ball; 14 WPI], 1 ball #NGO.4921 silver
- Set of four US 7 [4.5mm] double pointed needles
- US 7 [4.5mm] circular needle, 24in [60cm] long
- Set of four US 6 [4mm] double pointed needles
- 2 stitch markers
- Three sew-on silver snaps (size 3). Note: do not use black or coated snaps as these will not conduct electricity as well as bare metal snaps.
- Matching green sewing thread
- Large sewing needle

Additional Supplies for the eTextile option (supplies are not difficult to find—see Resources, page 189)

- 3 yds [2.7 m] of conductive thread
- 2 green LEDs
- 2 battery holders #BS7
- 2 coin batteries #CR2032
- 1 tube puffy fabric paint (white, light gray, or glow-in-the-dark)
- Small wire cutter
- Small round-nosed pliers

GAUGE
18 stitches and 24 rows = 4in [10 cm] in stockinette with MC and larger needles

PATTERN NOTES
This is a great project on which to practice buttonholes. If they don't turn out perfectly, it doesn't matter; they get covered up later by the neck bolts.

PATTERN BEGINS
Collar
The collar is worked in stockinette with a garter stitch border. Buttonholes on either side provide access to electronics hidden inside the neck bolts.

With MC and circular needle, cast on 65 [71] sts.
Rows 1-6: Knit.
Row 7 [WS]: K3, purl to last 3 sts, k3.
Row 8: Knit.
Rows 9-12: Rep Rows 7-8 twice more.
Row 13 (buttonhole row): K3, p11 [14], bind off 2 sts pwise, p33, bind off 2 sts pwise, p11 [14], k3.
Row 14: Knit, casting on 2 sts over each bound-off space.
Rows 15-20: Rep Rows 7-8 three times.
Row 21: K17 [20], p31, k17 [20].
Row 22: Knit.
Rows 23-24: Rep Rows 21-22.
Row 25: Rep Row 21.
Row 26: BO 14 [17], p3, knit to last 17 [20] sts, p3, bind off last 14 [17] sts. 37 sts remain.

Hood
Increasing up from the neck, the hood cups the back of the head until 1in [2.5cm] above eyebrow level, at which point it encircles the head.

Row 1 [RS]: Rejoin MC to the 37 sts rem on the needle. K9, M1R, k9, pm, M1R, k1, M1L, pm, k9, M1L, k9. 41 sts.
Row 2 [WS]: K3, purl to last 3 sts, k3.
Row 3: K9, M1R, k10, sl m, M1R, knit to next marker, M1L, sl m, k10, M1L, k to end. 45 sts.
Row 4: K3, purl to last 3 sts, k3.
Row 5: Knit to marker, sl m, M1R, knit to next marker, M1L, sl m, knit to end. 2 sts inc'd.
Rep Rows 4-5 six times more. 59 sts.
Change to CC1.
Rep Rows 4-5 six times more. 71 sts.
Work even in stockinette, maintaining garter borders, until hood reaches to 1in (2.5cm) above your eyebrows. End with a WS row.

Crown

Switch to larger dpn on next row as foll: k31 onto first needle, k31 onto second needle, k9 onto third needle, pm for border. Using cable or backward loop method, cast on an additional 22 sts to third needle. 93 sts in all. Pm for beg of rnd and join to work in the round.

Rnd 2: P3, knit to 3 sts before marker, p3, sl m, p22.

Rnd 3: Knit.

Rnd 4: Rep Rnd 2.

Rnd 5: P3, knit to end. (Note: This round adds an extra ridge of purls to the right side border of the hood, which hides the jog at the beginning of the rnd.)

Rnd 6: Rep Rnd 2.

Knit 9 rnds.

> **ON THE WWMDFK? WEBSITE:**
>
> *What could be better when galumphing about the alps than a nice, steaming crock of ale-rich fondue. Gluten-free beer still works, so don't hold back.*

Monstrous Bangs

The next round will be a purl row, to create the top line of a flat head, and you will create monstrous bangs every third stitch (or if you're feeling creative, as often or sparsely as you like.)

The bangs are created as follows:

1. Purl two stitches.
2. Pull up a 2in [5cm] long loop of yarn through the next stitch on the left needle.
3. Insert your finger in the loop and twist clockwise about 10-12 times.
4. Put the end of the loop on the left needle and allow the loop to ply back on itself. You may need to tug on the end of the plied loop to straighten it out.
5. Purl the end of the loop together with the next stitch on the left needle, making sure that the purling strand of yarn goes over the plied loop to push it down. This encourages the plied loop to hang down like hair, instead of sticking up like a tentacle.

Repeat steps 1-5 all the way around. 31 bang loops. Remove the markers as you come to them.

I first saw this plied-loop technique on Cat Bordhi's hat. She had learned the technique from Annie Modesitt. Cat briefly described how the method worked, but I had to go home and play with yarn to truly figure it out. So this is my interpretation of an Annie Modesitt technique as briefly explained by Cat Bordhi.

Crown Decreases

I wanted the top of the hat to be flat, to evoke the iconic Frankenstein's monster. Although the monster in the novel was described as having been created from a beautiful man with long flowing locks, Boris Karloff's interpretation for Universal Studios has created a lasting meme that can't be denied.

Knit around until you are at the center back stitch of the hood—35 sts from the beg of the rnd. Looking down at the gusset will help you make sure you're in the right place. Pm to indicate new beg of rnd.

Rnd 1: *K8, k2tog; rep from * to last 3 sts, k1, k2tog. 83 sts.
Rnd 2 and all even-numbered rnds: Knit.
Rnd 3: *K7, k2tog; rep from * to last 2 sts, k2tog. 73 sts.
Rnd 5: *K6, k2tog; rep from * to last 9 sts, k6, k3tog. 63 sts.
Rnd 7: *K5, k2tog; rep from * to end. 54 sts.
Rnd 9: *K4, k2tog; rep from * to end. 45 sts.
Rnd 11: *K3, k2tog; rep from * to end. 36 sts.
Rnd 13: *K2, k2tog; rep from * to end. 27 sts.
Rnd 15: *K1, k2tog; rep from * to end. 18 sts.
Rnd 17: *K2tog; rep from * to end. 9 sts.

Break yarn, leaving a 10in [25cm] tail. Thread the yarn tail onto a tapestry needle and pass through all the live stitches. Remove the needles and cinch tight. Pull the tail to the inside of the hood and weave in.

Tip: To get a truly tight gather at the top, pull the end again after it's been woven in.

Neck Bolts (make 2)
The hollow neck bolts cover the buttonholes and, in the eTextile version, hide the electronics.

Using the smaller dpn and CC2, cast on 12 stitches, leaving a 12in [30cm] tail. Join to knit in the round.
Rnds 1-4: Knit.
Rnd 5: *K1, m1; rep from * to end. 24 sts.
Rnd 6: Purl.
Rnds 7-9: *K5, p1; rep from * to end.
Rnd 10: Purl.
Rnd 11: *K2tog; rep from * to end. 12 sts.
Rnd 12: Knit.
Rnd 13: *K2tog; rep from * to end. 6 sts.

Cut yarn, thread tail on a tapestry needle and run through all the stitches. Pull tight to close, take the yarn to the inside of the neck bolt and weave in.

Using the long tails from the cast on, whipstitch the neck bolts to the collar over the buttonholes. When you are done, the buttonholes should not be visible from the outside of the hood and you should be able to poke your finger into the neck bolts from the inside.

Tip: To make sure you don't inadvertently sew the buttonhole closed, stick your finger through the button hole and into the bolt while you are sewing.

Finishing
Weave in ends. Block if desired. If you aren't adding the electronics, sew the snaps onto the collar now. If you are, don't attach the snaps just yet.

ADDING THE ELECTRONICS (OPTIONAL)

In this section, you'll add LEDs to the neck bolts, giving the hood an eerie glow and that last bit of verisimilitude.

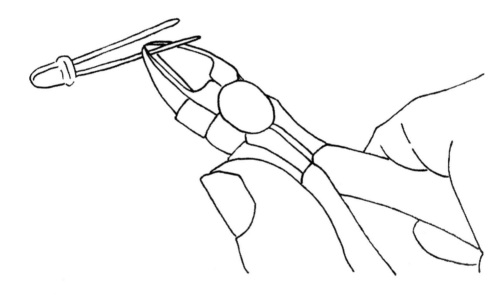

It's optional, but I encourage you to give it a go. Isn't experimenting with science and accepting that things may go horribly awry what the novel is all about? I mean, it's not like this pattern calls for digging up corpses. Get thee to Radio Shack and Sparkfun for a few notions and let's make this Frankenhood live!

Prepare the LED by trimming the long leg down to 1in [2.5cm], and the short leg down to 0.75in [2cm].

Note: It's important to maintain the long-short properties of the leg, because the long leg needs to go to the positive side of the battery, and the short leg needs to go to the negative side of the battery.

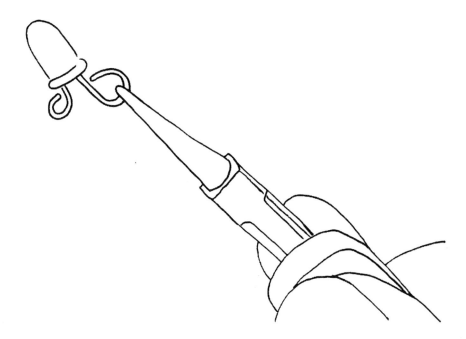

Using round-nose pliers, curl the LED's legs into sewable rings.

Cut the pointy leads off the bottom of the battery holder. Thread 18in [46cm] of conductive thread onto a needle and wrap it around the negative pole of the battery holder, as shown.

Turn the first neck bolt inside out. Use conductive thread to sew the negative pole to the center of the neck bolt, in much the same way as you would sew on a button.

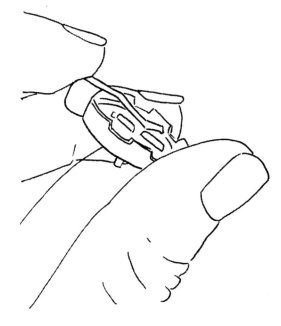

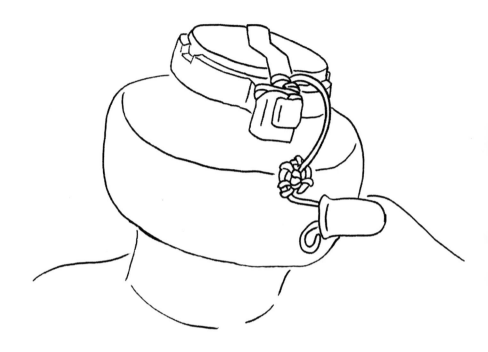

Sew the large loop of the LED to the positive pole of the battery with a short piece of conductive thread.

Using a new piece of conductive thread, sew on to the negative lead (small loop) of the LED.

Repeat for the second neck bolt.

Stitch the conductive thread to complete the circuit as shown in the diagram at right, sewing the conductive thread to the male and female halves of a snap centered in the collar, in the garter stitch borders.

Take care not to pull the stitches too tightly when sewing with the conductive thread or the knit fabric will pucker. Also be careful not to cross the negative (shown in green) and positive (shown in pink) traces. If you do, you'll create a short circuit and one or more of the LEDs may not light up.

I used a zig-zag stitch reminiscent of the stitching on the iconic Frankenstein monster.

After you have sewn the circuit above and verified that both LEDs are glowing, cover the conductive thread and knots inside the neck bolts with puffy fabric paint. The puffy fabric paint acts as an insulator and prevents the circuit from shorting out inside the neck bolt.

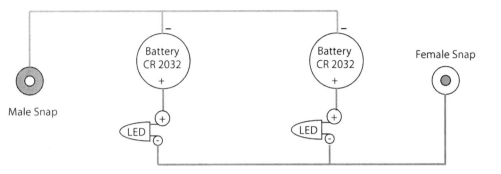

Allow the paint to dry fully, then invert the neck bolts so they are right side out again.

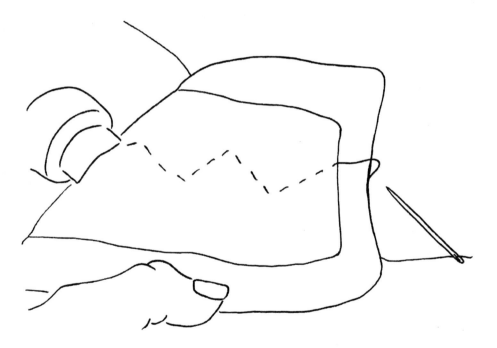

Use normal sewing thread in a coordinating green color to sew on two more snaps, one above and one below the snap sewn on with the conductive thread.

The middle snap now acts like a switch. Snapping it shut completes the circuit and causes the LEDs to light. Opening the snap turns off the lights.

The other two snaps are not "live" electronically, but simply help hold the collar on.

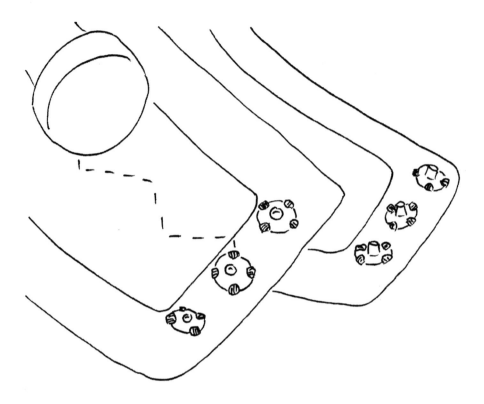

FRANKENCOLLAR

If you're just a titch monstrous, you can create the scaled-down Frankencollar. All of the eTextile fun, with a lot less knitting.

For this variation, simply replace rows 21-26 of the collar instructions with six rows of garter stitch, then bind off all. Work the neck bolts and add the electronics as described above.

E-TEXTILE SUPPLIES

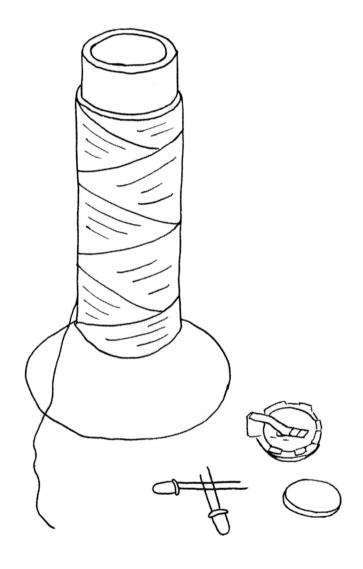

Colour Revolt Triangular Shawl(ette)

INTERLUDE II

Flatland: A Romance of Many Dimensions
Written and Illustrated by A. Square (Edwin Abbott Abbott)

Oh, *Flatland*. How I admire Heather Ordover for trying to bring your amazing existence to better understanding here in Spaceland. But oh, how you and your two-dimensional mental gymnastics make my head hurt. I tried, I really, really tried to plow through this mathematically-based, Victorian era social satire with pen and paper in hand, doodling to try to make sense of what I was hearing…and then reading as my brain couldn't keep up. Eventually, I gave up totally and completely and simply listened.

Not that this difficulty came as any surprise to me. I'm the kid who blew through Algebra, Geometry and Trig only to start my junior year of high school by slamming up against the brick wall of Calculus. My brain just does not bend that way. I like concrete. I like representational. I like intuitive. And I really, really like my box. There comes a point when math starts getting hinky and starts pushing the bounds of what I can see, hear and feel; and that's when I step back sadly and let others get on with things. Totally buggered my grand sci-fi driven plans to become a brilliant research scientist, deep space astronomer, or quantum physicist.

<insert SIGH here>

So I was fairly certain that *Flatland* was going to be a chore. I did fairly well for a bit. Women: straight lines. Don't like it, but got it. Soldiers and working classes: acute triangles. Got it. Middle class: equilateral triangles. Got it. Professionals and gentlemen: squares and pentagons. Got it. Nobility and priests: polygons and circles. Got it. Maybe this isn't going to be so bad.

Then, as feared, things went hinky. Housing, methods of identification, and then delving into Spaceland (3D), Pointland (0D), and Lineland (1D) from a 2D perspective… AHHHHHHH! Not surprising then that the discussion of color nabbed my attention.

I speak now from the aesthetic and artistic point of view when I say that life with us is dull; aesthetically and artistically, very dull indeed.

How can it be otherwise, when all one's prospect, all one's landscapes, historical pieces, portraits, flowers, still life, are nothing but a single line, with no varieties except degrees of brightness and obscurity?

It was not always thus. Colour[2], if Tradition speaks the truth, once for the space of half a

---

2 — *Yep. We know. But that's how Edwin Abbott Abbott spelled it, and it's his party.*

dozen centuries or more, threw a transient splendour over the lives of our ancestors in the remotest ages. Some private individual – a Pentagon whose name is variously reported – having casually discovered the constituents of the simpler colours and a rudimentary method of painting, is said to have begun decorating first his house, then his slaves, then his Father, his Sons, and Grandsons, lastly himself. The convenience as well as the beauty of the results commended themselves to all. Wherever Chromatistes – for by that name the most trustworthy authorities concur in calling him – turned his variegated frame, there he at once excited attention, and attracted respect. No one now needed to "feel" him; no one mistook his front for his back; all his movements were readily ascertained by his neighbours without the slightest strain on their powers of calculation; no one jostled him, or failed to make way for him; his voice was saved the labour of that exhausting utterance by which we colourless Squares and Pentagons are often forced to proclaim our individuality when we move amid a crowd of ignorant Isosceles.

Okay! Now they're talking my language. Images of triangles and polygons with sides of various hues replaced the pain of 2D manipulations. I loved how the use of language changed in these passages, the vocabulary richer and more varied along with the subject matter. Emotion almost drips off the page in these sections, markedly different from the cool analysis found elsewhere. The concept of color influencing language and thought and expression, then all continuing to evolve together to enrich life…fantastic, though apparently short lived.

Immoral, licentious, anarchical, unscientific – call them by what names you will – yet, from an aesthetic point of view, those ancient days of the Colour Revolt were the glorious childhood of Art in Flatland – a childhood, alas, that never ripened into manhood, nor even reached the blossom of youth.

…Year by year the Soldiers and Artisans began more vehemently to assert – and with increasing truth – that there was no great difference between them and the very highest class of Polygons. …they began to insist that inasmuch as Colour, which was a second Nature, had destroyed the need of aristocratic distinctions, the Law should follow in the same path, and that henceforth all individuals and all classes should be recognized as absolutely equal and entitled to equal rights.

Sadly, we find an age-old tale spinning itself out once again. Rigid social caste structure, glimmer of progress, growing dissent, open rebellion. In this Victorian-tinged instance, all does not end well for the masses. It doesn't take long for the less virtuous to figure out how to exploit the camouflaging opportunities now available to them. The Colour Revolt and its ill-conceived Colour Bill inevitably fall to the folly of fraud and domestic strife, ending in one glorious rhetoric-inflamed battle that enabled the wholesale slaughter of the lower classes.

The Circles delayed not to push their victory to the uttermost. The Working Men they spared but decimated. The Militia of the Equilaterals was at once called out; and every Triangle suspected of Irregularity on reasonable grounds, was destroyed by Court Martial, without the formality of exact measurement by the Social Board. The homes of the Military and Artisan classes were inspected in a course of visitations extending through upwards of a year; and during that period every town, village, and hamlet was systematically purged of that excess of the lower orders which had been brought about by the neglect to pay the tribute of Criminals to the Schools and University, and by the violation of the other natural Laws of the Constitution of Flatland. Thus the balance of classes was again restored.

Needless to say that henceforth the use of Colour was abolished, and its possession prohibited. ...Colour is now non-existent. The art of making it is known to only one living person, the Chief Circle for the time being; and by him it is handed down on his deathbed to none but his Successor. One manufactory alone produces it; and, lest the secret should be betrayed, the Workmen are annually consumed, and fresh ones introduced. So great is the terror with which even now our Aristocracy looks back to the far distant days of the agitation for the Universal Colour Bill.

Sound familiar? Seeing any parallels here?

Need I spell out what Madame Defarge would knit in *Flatland*? No, I didn't think so.

Vive la révolution!

— Dawn

COLOUR REVOLT TRIANGULAR SHAWL(ETTE)
Designed by Dawn Ellerd

Flatland gave me a raging case of triangles on the brain. I became infatuated with the idea of colors camouflaging their dimensions and measurements in 2D. When talking yarn, the effect created by the application of color of course depends on how that triangle is created, and becomes even more heightened when viewed in 3D, which in turn reveals the triangle's inner structure. Therefore I give you 3 recipes for creating your own legion of triangle warriors and the necessary tools to vary their dimensions. Long live the Colour Revolt!

FINISHED MEASUREMENTS
Triangles with sides measuring approx. 70in x 45in x 45in [178cm x 114.5cm 114.5cm] using 2 skeins in stitch patterns shown below.

MATERIALS

- Noro Kureyon Sock [70% wool/30% nylon; 462yd/422m 100g skein; 14 WPI], 1-2 skeins. Shown: #180 (shawl 1), #185 (shawl 2), #150 (shawl 3)
- US H [5mm] crochet hook

GAUGE

Not critical to this project. Adjust hook size to suit your yarn and achieve the fabric you desire.

Liberté

PATTERN NOTES

- Using the patterns as written, 2 skeins of Noro Sock will be needed for a functionally sized triangular shawl/scarf. If you modify to create a very acute/narrow triangle, 1 may suffice.
- With this yarn, I highly recommend you wash and vigorously block your shawl to open the stitches and give good drape. In my experience, the Kureyon Sock blooms and softens dramatically with each washing.
- These triangles all have two equilateral sides and one long side. The angle opposite the long side is referred to as "the point."
- Generic instructions and one stitch pattern variation are given for each construction method. Generic instructions will result in a shawl of solid double crochet fabric.

PATTERN BEGINS

Construction 1: Point on Up

Accomplished by starting with a few stitches at the point and inserting increases along both edges. This shawl grows in a "v" shape, from the point up and outward.

START

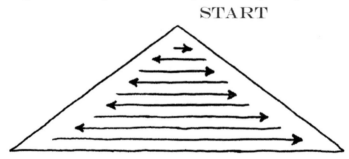

Generic

Row1: Ch4 (counts as 1 ch + 1 dc), dc3 in 4th ch from hook. 4 sts.

Row2: Ch3 (counts as 1 dc), turn. Dc2 at base of turning ch, dc across, dc3 in last stitch. 4 sts inc'd.

Repeat Row 2 until it's as big a shawl/scarf as you like. Break yarn, tie off and weave ends.

Granny Variation

Row 1: Ch4 (counts as 1 ch + 1 dc), dc3 in 4th ch from hook. 4 sts.

Row 2: Ch3 (counts as 1 dc), turn. Dc2 at base of turning ch. Dc3 (shell) in space between 2nd and 3rd dc of previous row, dc3 in last stitch. 3 shells.

Row 3: Ch3, turn. Dc2 at base of turning chain. Work across row placing 3dc shells in spaces between shells of previous row. Dc3 in last stitch.

Repeat Row 3 until it's as big a shawl/scarf as you like. Break yarn, tie off and weave ends.

Modifications

You can narrow or deepen your "v" by modifying either the number of stitches in each increase or the frequency of those increases.

For example, to make a wider "V", place more than 3 stitches in the increases at the beginning and end of the row. There is a limit to this technique however. At some point, the arms of the "v" will start to curve.

To make a narrower, pointier "V", do not increase every row. Instead, insert an "even" row or 2 in between, like so: Ch3, turn. Dc across row. Dc1 in last stitch. Warning: when working in dc, things get to look "stair steppy" with more than one or two even rows between increases. Sc gives you a bit more latitude as the stitches aren't as tall.

Stitch patterns and charted patterns are easily inserted in this construction by maintaining the integrity of the increases at each edge…think of them as selvedge stitches…stitches outside of the body of your scarf. They sit here in the gutter until needed for an additional pattern repeat.

Construction 2: Acute Angle to Acute Angle

Accomplished by starting with a few stitches at the angle at one end of the long side, increasing along one edge while working even along the other, then switching to decreases

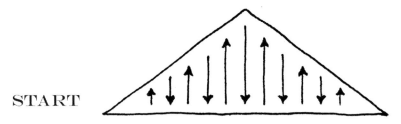

START

once the desired depth of shawl/scarf has been reached.

With this construction, it is very helpful to weigh your yarn before beginning. You can then determine when you have used half of the weight in the increase section and therefore have the same amount left for the second half of the shawl. Do not think that because you have two skeins things will work out…skeins can vary. Save yourself some heartache just a few rows from finishing and weigh them both now!

Generic
Row 1: Ch4 (counts as 1 ch + 1 dc), dc2 in 4th ch from hook. 3 sts.
Row 2: Ch3 (counts as 1 dc), turn. Dc2 at base of turning ch, dc to end of row. 2 sts inc'd.
Row 3: Ch3 (counts as 1 dc), turn. Dc across row, dc3 in last st. 2 sts inc'd.
Repeat Rows 2-3 until it's as deep a shawl/scarf as you like, or half of yarn is used. End with Row 3.
Row 4: Ch 3, turn. Dc2tog, dc to end of row.
Row 5: Ch 3, turn. Dc across row to last 3 stitches. Dc2tog, dc in last st.
Repeat Rows 4-5 until only 3 stitches remain. Break yarn, tie off and weave ends.

Grid variation
Row 1: Ch4 (counts as 1 ch + 1 dc), dc2 in 4th ch from hook. 3 sts.
Row 2: Ch1, sc across.
Row 3: Ch4 (counts as 1 dc + 1 ch), turn. Dc at base of tc. *Ch1, skip 1 st, dc in next st. Repeat from * across. 2 sts inc'd.
Repeat Rows 2-3 until it's as deep a shawl/scarf as you like. End with Row 3.
Row 4: Ch1, sc across.
Row 5: Ch2, skip 1 st, dc in next st. *Ch1, skip 1 st, dc in next st. Repeat from * across. 2 sts dec'd.
Row 6: Ch1, sc across. (Make sure your last sc is in the dc, not the turning ch).
Repeat Rows 5 -6 until only 3 stitches remain. Dc3tog. Break yarn, tie off and weave ends.

Modifications
This construction gets long and skinny very easily by, again, varying the number of even rows between increase and decrease rows. After some point though, you again stop getting a smooth increase or decrease and end up with steps. Not that there's anything wrong with that. Steps are nice too.
Basic stitch combos are easily inserted in this pattern. 2-3 stitch combos work best as each increase can easily add those stitches for an additional repeat.

If you're after a more complex charted pattern though, you'll have to do a bit of planning as you increase and decrease to maintain symmetry. In this case, I recommend having 2-4 stitches worked plainly at each edge to accommodate the increases without goofing with your pattern. As with the first, these additional stitches just hang about until there are enough of them to give you an additional repeat of your chart.

Construction 3: The Miter
Accomplished by starting with a few stitches at the center of the longest edge, then increasing at each end and along the center line.

Generic
Row 1: Ch4 (counts as 1 ch + 1 dc), [dc2, ch1, dc3] in 4th ch from hook. This creates a cluster of [dc3, ch1, dc3] that will continue upward as the point of the shawl.
Row 2: Ch3 (counts as 1 dc), turn. Dc2 at base of turning ch, dc across first side of triangle to center ch1 space, [dc3, ch1, dc3] in center ch space, dc across second side, dc3 in last st.

10 sts inc'd.
Repeat Row 2 until you have the shawl/scarf you'd like or your yarn is gone. Break yarn, tie off, weave in ends.

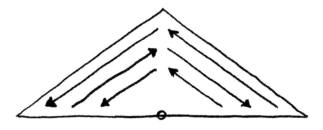

START

V-stitch Variation

Row 1: Ch4 (counts as 1 ch + 1 dc), [dc2, ch1, dc3] in 4th ch from hook. This creates a cluster of [dc3, ch, dc3] that will continue upward as the point of the shawl.

Row 2: Ch4, turn, dc at base of turning ch (counts as 1 V-stitch). [Dc3, ch1, dc3] in center sp, [dc, ch1, dc] in last st (1 V-stitch made). 2 V-stitches and 1 [dc3, ch1, dc3] cluster.

Row3: Ch4, turn. Dc at base of turning ch, [dc, ch, dc] between V-stitches (not in the center of the V-stitch) along 1st side. [dc3, ch1, dc3] in center space, [dc, ch, dc] between v-stitches along 2nd side and in last stitch. 2 V-stitches and 6 dc inc'd.

Repeat Row 3 until you have the shawl/scarf you'd like or your yarn is gone. Break yarn, tie off, weave in ends.

Modifications

This construction can easily give you a curved or winged effect by adding additional stitches to the edge increases.

You can easily play with the center angle as well. More stitches in the center increases will give you a narrower point and deeper, more dramatic "V," fewer, and the center angle opens up, creating a shallower "V."

This center increase also gives you a place to get creative. Think about using a different pattern here…work a solid shell, chain every other stitch, or insert one of the many floral or leaf patterns along the center line for some drama.

On the WWMDfK? website:

You didn't think we'd be able to come up with a recipe for Flatland, *did you? How about this? Swedish Pancakes! About the flattest food you can get that's still delicious!*

SONG OF THE SEA

Jack Sparrow is not the only reason to harbor a love of the sea. There is nothing quite like being lulled to sleep at night by the pounding surf and the rasp of the water on the craggy Cornwall shore. Misty mornings walking in the night-warm sand of the Pacific, or listening for foghorns off the Atlantic can set you in a mood for mystery or adventure. It is no wonder that so many legends and stories have centered on the ocean.

I was lucky enough to spend my childhood summers at a beachside town that didn't know the 60s and 70s had happened — rare in Southern California. From the Fun Zone, with its chocolate-dipped frozen bananas, to the Crab Cooker's red Manhattan Chowder, the whole summer — every summer — was enchanted. And ever since then, living land-locked has cast a special type of melancholy on me during the month of August.

And it's not just the humidity.

The beauty and mystery of the ocean has been the focus of song and legend for as long as we've had songs and legends. In the Western Canon, some of our most epic stories center on the sea quest, as in Moby Dick. Some address the unaccountable mystery the sea offers us, the "Call of Cthulhu" being just one example, and some… well some are just downright wacky like "The Rime of the Ancient Mariner." So grab some wool (if you aren't allergic…or maybe a nice seacell blend if you are) and knit some sea-worthy socks, scarves and caps. Sheep know what they're doing when it comes to the damp. And who knows — maybe Cthulhu wouldn't have been so scary if his tentacles had been warm!

Cthulhu

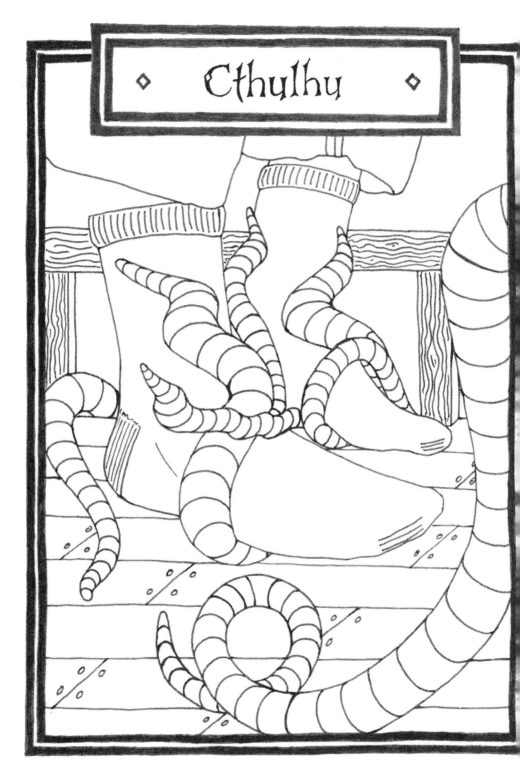

THE CALL OF CTHULHU
H. P. Lovecraft

When I heard about this book, I instantly knew I wanted to be a part of it. Figuring out just exactly what I wanted to make took quite a bit longer. Well, I knew I wanted to make socks (I nearly always want to make socks) but not which literary character I wanted to draw them from.

I have to confess that I'm not a big fan of classic literature. Heresy, I know. It's not that I don't like to read or that I dislike the past. Far from it. The only rooms in my house that don't have bookcases in them are the bathroom and the dining room, and my day job (should I ever finish this blasted degree) will be as a historian. It's just that I can't often seem to find the nice long stretches of uninterrupted time required to properly immerse myself in classic literature. That's one of the reasons the CraftLit podcast is so marvelous. But I didn't want to do something from one of the books covered on the show. Somehow that felt like cheating. It seemed important to work with something I'd actually held in my hands and read.

I considered doing something from one of the Icelandic sagas. The idea of scads of tiny cables was intriguing, but most of the characters in the sagas are too busy cleaving each other with axes to feel properly knit-worthy. My next thought was something from the short stories of Somerset Maugham. Alas, copyright issues make this one a bit tricky. (Perhaps I'll revisit the idea for a second volume.) I started to get worried. I should have known better.

A few days later, I stopped by my favorite used bookstore for a bit of a ramble. I wasn't even thinking about the project. The store is eclectic and employs a rather freeform organizational scheme. You're sure to find something marvelous, but there's absolutely no telling what it will be. I was exploring the new arrivals area when I stumbled — literally stumbled — over a pile of books. I dusted myself off and looked to see what I'd tripped on. It was a collection of H. P. Lovecraft's stories. I was thunderstruck. By the time I'd tidied up the books, I knew exactly what I wanted to do.

I've always had a bit of a soft spot for Lovecraft, and "The Call of Cthulhu" is a particular favorite. Lovecraft somehow manages to be both genuinely disconcerting and oddly amusing at the same time. I have no idea how something written in such unabashedly florid prose can be both creepy and endearing, but it manages. It's full of "sky-flung monoliths, all dripping with green ooze and sinister with latent horror," yet the whole is unreasonably affecting.

The story told in "The Call of Cthulhu" is almost absurdly simple. It is framed as a manuscript, "found among the papers of the late Francis Wayland Thurston" telling of Thurston's discovery of notes collected by his recently deceased great-uncle, Professor

George Gammell Angell. These notes hint at the existence of an ancient cult dedicated to worshiping the Great Old Ones, Cthulhu among them, and waiting for them to awaken from their deathless sleep under the seas and beyond the stars and bring the world once more under their terrible sway. Thurston, an anthropologist, becomes obsessed with this cult and travels the world hoping to learn more about it, a course of action which he fears may well result in his own death.

Nothing is resolved. The story is never neatly summed up. The cult is never explained; nor are the Old Ones. Cthulhu himself makes only the briefest appearance, and that only in the account of a terrified, traumatized sailor. Cthulhu is never fully described, for "there is no language for such abysms of shrieking and immemorial lunacy, such eldritch[3] contradictions of all matter, force, and cosmic order." He is said only to be a "green, sticky, spawn of the stars," a "mountainous monstrosity" topped by an "awful squid-head with writhing feelers." The whole story is only a few dozen pages long and feels like a tiny snippet of a larger work.

Perhaps this incompleteness is part of the story's appeal. Lovecraft used elements of the Cthulhu mythos in many of his other works. Members of his circle of friends expanded on it in their writing with Lovecraft's knowledge and enthusiastic consent. Lovecraft's writing in general, and the Cthulhu mythos in particular continue to inspire modern creative work and have been cited as influential by people like Stephen King, Peter Straub, Neil Gaiman, Alan Moore, and Guillermo Del Toro. It's even spawned several games, toys, podcasts, and countless modern parodies.

Despite being a part of popular culture now, there is still something in the original that is faintly unsettling. The cuddly cartoon Cthulhu dolls feel somehow like whistling past the graveyard. I wanted to make something that hinted at the more sinister nature of Lovecraft's Cthulhu. While he is never clearly described, statues and carvings of him do feature in the tale. The first "yielded simultaneous pictures of an octopus, a dragon, and a human caricature... A pulpy, tentacled head surmounted a grotesque and scaly body with rudimentary wings; but it was the general outline of the whole which made it most shockingly frightful." The second "represented a monster of vaguely anthropoid outline, but with an octopus-like head whose face was a mass of feelers." Tentacles feature prominently in all the descriptions, and so became the inspiration for this sock. With luck, they'll add an ever so slightly disquieting note to your knitting.

— Hunter

---

3 — *eldritch: strangely ghostly and unearthly*

CTHULHU WAITS
Designed by Hunter Hammersen

I am shamefully easily amused. It's really quite embarrassing. Tentacles are high on the list of things that entertain me. They manage to be both fascinating and just a wee bit frightening. These socks are just swimming in tentacles. They creep up over the top of your foot and wrap stealthily around your ankle.

Don't let the charts scare you away. They look much harder than they actually are. Once you've done the first few rounds, all you have to do is note what happens on the edges of the tentacles and knit blithely away for the rest of the round.

I strongly recommend cabling without a cable needle. It's a skill worth mastering if it's not already in your repertoire, and it will make these socks much quicker. None of these cables are large, which makes them easy to work without a cable needle.

SIZE
One size fits most women

FINISHED MEASUREMENTS
Foot circumference 8in [20.5cm]

MATERIALS
- Briar Rose Fibers Grandma's Blessing [100% superwash merino; 600 yds/546m per 180g skein, 16 WPI], 1 skein (please note: this yarn is dyed in one of a kind lots, and there is no color name)
- Set of four or five US 1 [2.25mm] double pointed needles or circulars for your preferred method of sock knitting
- Cable needle (optional)
- Stitch markers

GAUGE
32 sts = 4in [10cm] in stockinette

PATTERN NOTES

This pattern lends itself to dpns or any other needle combination you enjoy. Please be sure to check your gauge as knitting in cables may alter your normal tension.

To adjust the size of the sock, adjust the thickness of your yarn and thus your gauge. In a standard sock yarn worked at 32 stitches per 4in [10cm], the sock will be approximately 8 inches [20.5cm] around. In a slightly thicker sock yarn worked at 30 stitches per 4in [10cm], the sock will be approximately 8.75 inches [22.5cm] around. In a slightly thinner sock yarn worked at 35 stitches per 4in [10cm], the sock will be approximately 7.25 inches [18.5cm] around.

There are several 'bubbles' sprinkled throughout the pictured sock. They are optional, and their placement is random. If you wish to use them, they are made like this:

1. Work along until you come to an area of plain knit stitches where you would like a bubble.
2. Knit the next stitch, wrapping your yarn 5 times around your needle.
3. Finish the round as shown on the chart.
4. When you come to that stitch in the next round, drop 2 of the wraps to free up some yarn.
5. Work your needle into the remaining wraps from right to left and knit them together through the back loop.

If you would like a taller sock you can work extra rounds of ribbing, work extra rounds of plain knitting before starting the chart, or repeat any of the shaded rounds on the chart once or twice. If you choose to repeat the rounds, be sure to do so on both Charts A and B.

On Chart C, the last stitches on Rnds 24 and 42 and the first stitches on Rnds 32 and 41 require extra attention. These stitches take the tentacles off the edges of the top of your foot. These cables involve the last stitch on the top of the foot and the first stitch on the bottom of the foot. They are worked in the usual way, just over a stitch that isn't normally considered part of the top of the foot.

PATTERN BEGINS

Cuff

Using a stretchy method, cast on 64 sts. Sts 1-32 are the front of the sock, sts 33-64 are the back of the sock. Place markers or divide sts across needles to distinguish front and back. If you use markers, slip them whenever you come to them. The socks are mirrored. Be sure you're following the appropriate (left or right) charts.

> **CABLING WITHOUT A CABLE NEEDLE:**
> *If you would like a gander at a cabling-without-a-cable needle tutorial, Grumperina's is good. (http://www.grumperina.com/cables.htm)*

Rnd 1: *K1 tbl, p1; rep from * to end.
Rep Rnd 1 seven times more.

Leg

Knit 6 rnds.
Work the 47 rnds of the appropriate Charts A and B. Chart A is for the front of the sock, and B for the back. If you use markers, remove them before working the heel flap.

Heel Flap

The heel is worked over sts 33-64. Place the other sts on hold.
Row 1 [WS]: [Sl1 pwise wyif, p1] sixteen times.
Row 2 [RS]: Sl1 pwise wyib, knit to end.

Rep Rows 1-2 a total of sixteen times (32 rows).

Heel Turn
Row 1 [WS]: Sl1, p18, p2tog, p1, turn.

Row 2 [RS]: Sl1, k7, ssk, k1, turn.
Row 3: Sl1, p8, p2tog, p1, turn.
Row 4: Sl1, k9, ssk, k1, turn.
Row 5: Sl1, p10, p2tog, p1, turn.
Row 6: Sl1, k11, ssk, k1, turn.
Row 7: Sl1, p12, p2tog, p1, turn.
Row 8: Sl1, k13, ssk, k1, turn.
Row 9: Sl1, p14, p2tog, p1, turn.
Row 10: Sl1, k15, ssk, k1, turn.
Row 11: Sl1, p16, p2tog, p1.
Row 12: Sl1, k17, ssk, k1.
20 sts remain.

> **ON THE WWMDFK? WEBSITE:**
>
> *Feeling a little intimidated by the tentacles? Find your strength by devouring Cthulhu Destroyer of Pot Pies while listening to the Cthulhu podcast.*

Gusset
Rnd 1: Pick up and knit slipped sts (16 in this example) along right side of heel flap, pm. You can use the change from one dpn to another in lieu of markers. Work across held instep sts following Rnd 1 of Chart C. With another needle, pm, pick up and knit slipped sts (16 in this example) along left side of heel flap, then k10 sts from heel. The round now begins in the middle of the sole.
Rnd 2: Knit to 2 sts before first marker, k2tog, sl m. Work in patt to second marker, sl m, ssk, knit to end. 2 sts dec'd.
Rnd 3: Knit to first marker, work in patt to second marker, knit to end.
Rep Rnds 2-3 until 64 sts rem.

Foot
Work even in stockinette over sole and patt over instep to end of Chart C, then repeat Chart C Rnds 43-48 until foot measures desired length, less 2in [5cm] for toe shaping.

Toe
Rnd 1: Knit all sts.
Rnd 2: Knit to 3 sts before first marker, k2tog, k1, sl m, k1, ssk, knit to 3 sts before second marker, k2tog, k1, sl m, k1, ssk, knit to end. 4 sts dec'd.
Rep Rnds 1-2 five times more, then Rnd 2 only until 16 sts rem.
Graft rem sts together. Weave in ends.

CHART A LEFT

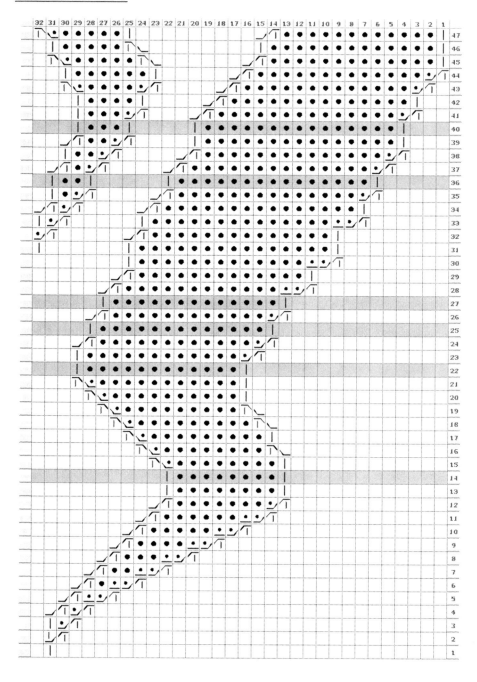

CHART A RIGHT

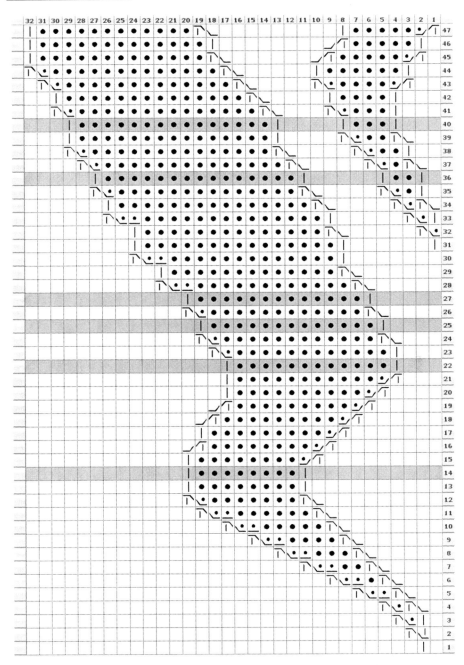

CHART B LEFT

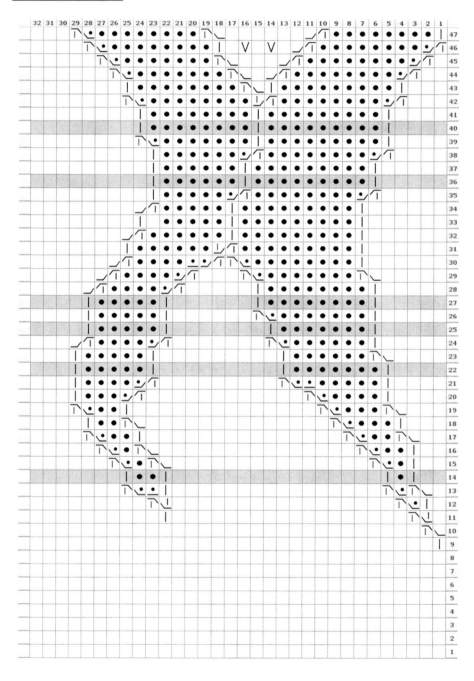

Chart B right

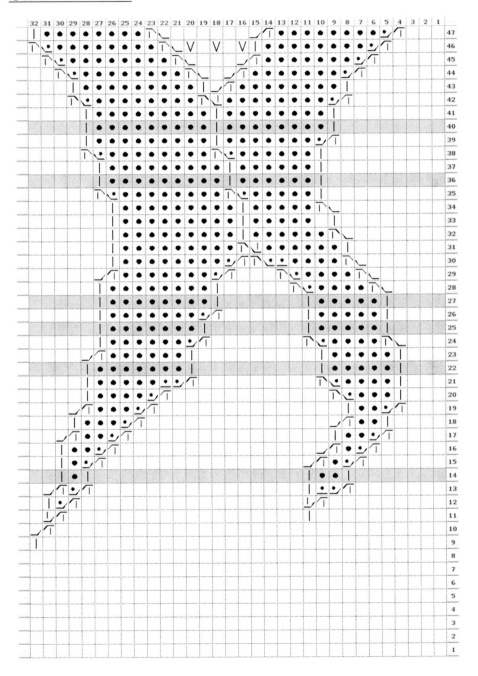

Again, please note (full explanation on page 100) that on Chart C, the last stitches on Rnds 24 and 42 and the first stitches on Rnds 32 and 41 require extra attention.

CHART C LEFT

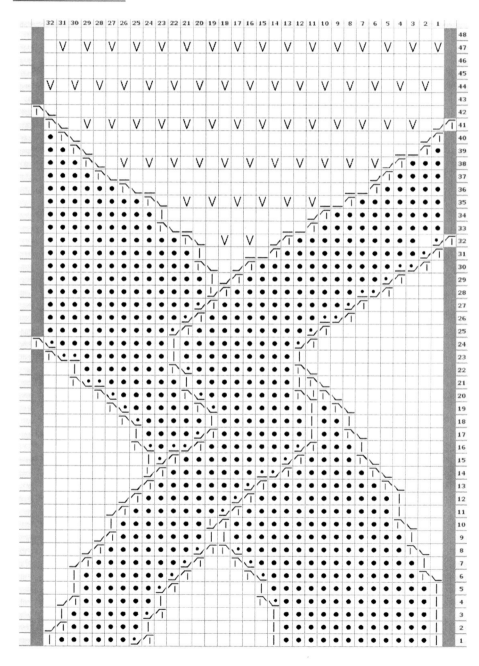

CHART C RIGHT

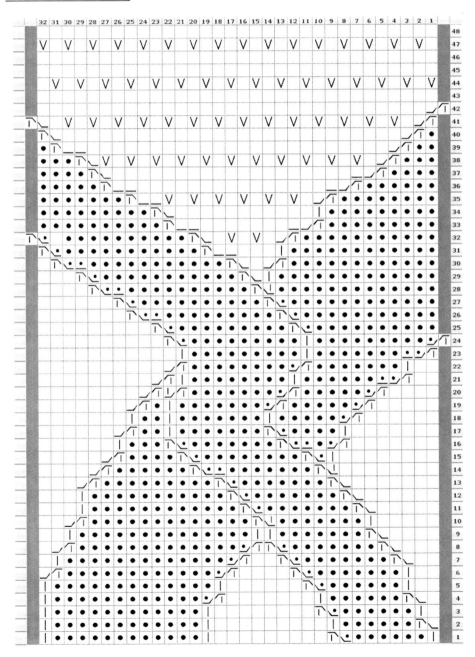

The White Wool

MOBY DICK
Herman Melville

"...he has a wife - not three voyages wedded - a sweet, resigned girl. Think of that; by that sweet girl that old man has a child...."
—Moby Dick, Chapter 16

This scarf is my husband's fault... I mean he gets the credit for this idea. We were discussing over dinner that *WWMDfK?* needed more men's patterns, when he said, "Remember that seaman's scarf you made me? You should do one for Captain Ahab," and The White Wool was born. Having read *Moby Dick* twice in college, however, I refused to read the entire book again. I refused. Call me lazy if you like, but I'm not gonna read it; if you want to read it, *vaya con Dios*. I won't stop you. Me? I'd rather knit a queen-sized afghan out of four colors of acrylic/wool blend. In the summer. For three months. With a deadline.*

Originally, I wanted to use a cool cable pattern that resembled a whale's tail, but a) it was quite fiddly, b) it would not have been reversible, and c) Ahab really wouldn't have cared. After all, this is the guy who got so riled up, he took off his hat, threw it into the water, and never retrieved it. He might have worn a scarf, but only out of necessity. Ahab was so focused on his quest that he would have barely noticed that he was wearing a scarf, much less some fancy cable pattern his young wife knit into it. So, here is a practical, simple seaman's scarf for Captain Ahab...or for someone in your life who needs a scarf but really wouldn't notice the effort put into a complicated Aran pattern knit in fingering weight wool. This is also a fairly quick knit, ideal for those "OOOPS, I forgot Uncle Queequeg's birthday and it's next weekend" moments. Enjoy, and watch out for those white whales; they're mean dudes.

— Erica

* *It should be noted that soon after I wrote the initial paragraphs, I got sick and had energy for little more than lolling in bed. In desperation, I picked up none other than Moby Dick to keep me company. (At my age, I should know better than to say "never" because I always end up having to cross those lines). Once I was feeling better, I fell asleep every time I tried to read the book. Apparently, I can only read Moby Dick when I'm ill. I wonder what that says about me?*

ON THE WWMDfK? WEBSITE:

Right about here is where you should be getting a hankerin' for a nice bowl of steaming soup...click over to the website for Ahab's Chowder.

THE WHITE WOOL
Designed by Erica Hernandez

WHAT WOULD MRS. AHAB KNIT? I picture Mrs. Ahab lovingly knitting gorgeous, ornate pieces for Ahab when they courted and for the first voyage after they got married. By the third voyage, between having a small child and seeing Ahab's, ahem, less than ideal treatment of his handknits, things would have changed. Hand-dye some fleece with indigo she'd grown in their yard, then spin a perfectly-balanced two-ply fingering-weight yarn and knit a scarf with complicated Celtic cables? Why bother when the man's probably just going to chuck it in the ocean at some whale? I wonder if Mrs. Ahab knit a handful of hats and scarves for each voyage so that there would be more waiting in his cabin for him if he got frustrated and flung his woolies into the deep.

Again.

I picture the scarves getting simpler and shorter with each voyage. "Sweet, resigned girl," indeed.

By the time Ahab shipped out this time, Mrs. Ahab would have wanted to knit him a plain garter stitch scarf. Knowing, however, that Ahab's knitwear would be her only representation on board the ship, she would have felt the need to do something a tad fancier than that, though. (C'mon, if your husband was the boss at his workplace and his co-workers only knew you through the hand knits he wore, wouldn't you want them to look good?) Hence, we have Ahab's Scarf: a garter stitch seaman's scarf with three reversible cables, knit in natural, undyed, "sheepy" wool. It's simple enough that Mrs. Ahab wouldn't have been heartbroken if Ahab threw it in the ocean, but has enough interest so that she wouldn't be mind-numbingly bored knitting it. The reversible cables are narrow enough that they are easy to knit without a cable needle, which is a plus when you've got an active toddler running around, getting into things, and putting everything in his mouth. Who needs to worry about whether Junior ate your cable needle — or shoved it up his nose? The pattern is forgiving, too. Cross your cable on the wrong row? No worries. Accidentally knit too many rows between cables? No problem! Just end it when you run out of yarn, even if you haven't run out of chart yet; Ahab won't care.

Knit one of these for your favorite obsessed whaleboat captain...or electronics technician...or professor...or retiree...or....

FINISHED MEASUREMENTS
7.5in x 70in [19cm x 178cm]

MATERIALS
- Fibranatura Shepherd's Own [100% wool, 252 yds/230m per 100g skein; 9 WPI], 2 skeins in #40001 Natural
- US 7 [4.5mm] needles
- Cable needle (optional)

GAUGE
24 sts and 40 rows = 4in [10cm] in pattern

STITCH GUIDE
4x4 Rib (multiple of 8 sts + 4)
Row 1: Sl1, k3, *p4, k4; rep from * to end.
Row 2: Sl1, p3, *k4, p4; rep from * to end.
Rep Rows 1-2.

Liberté

PATTERN BEGINS
Cast on 44 sts.

First End
Rows 1-6 [plain row]: [K8, k1, p1, k1, p1] three times, k8.
Row 7 [cable row]: [K8, sl2 to cable needle and hold to front, k1, p1, (k1, p1) from cable needle] three times, k8.
Work Rows 1-7 a total of five times.
Work 68 Plain Rows.
Work 1 Cable Row.
Work 17 Plain Rows.
Work 1 Cable Row.
Work 51 Plain Rows.
Work 1 Cable Row.
Work 51 Plain rows.
Knit 4 rows.

Center Section
Work in 4x4 Rib for 16in [40.5cm].

Second End
Knit 4 rows.
Work 51 Plain Rows.
Work 1 Cable Row.
Work 51 Plain Rows.
Work 1 Cable Row.
Work 17 Plain Rows.
Work 1 Cable Row.
Work 68 Plain Rows.
Work 1 Cable Row.
Work Rows 1-7 four times, then Rows 1-6 once.
Bind off knitwise.

Weave in ends. Block if desired. (*Ahab won't notice if you don't, though.*)

Ancient Mariner
Watch Cap

RIME OF THE ANCIENT MARINER
Samuel Taylor Coleridge

Stories have always fascinated me. Not only stories I read in books, but also the stories I would make my younger brother tell me when we were growing up. My husband tells the best stories about people passing by in airports and this is one of the things I adore about him. To this day I am enthralled by traditional storytellers like Norman Kennedy of the Scottish tradition and Charlotte Ross of the Appalachian tradition. Stories with incredible descriptive equality, surprise endings, a touch of irony and a bit of the macabre are those that attract me. For this reason, the following poem was right up my alley!

I love this poem for the fantastic way that Coleridge paints a mood with words and the intense, creepy scenes in which he has the mariner tell his tale. The old seaman in this poem detains a young gentleman anxiously making his way to a wedding and tells him the tale of a horrid, life–changing voyage to the Southern Hemisphere. After the mariner shot an albatross that had been following the ship and had been a pet to the crew, the ship lost wind for the sails and the crew ran out of supplies and began to die of thirst.

Day after day, day after day,
We stuck, nor breath nor motion;
As idle as a painted ship
Upon a painted ocean.

Water, water, every where,
And all the boards did shrink;
Water, water, every where,
Nor any drop to drink.

After all of the crew but himself passed away and the seaman suffered through many horrific visions, he learned to appreciate the beauty of sea snakes in the moon light. He was absolved for the murder of the albatross, was allowed once again to pray, and fell asleep. During the night it rained and, finally, he got something to drink. Angels then reanimated the corpses of his dead crew members and they assisted him in sailing the ship back to his home port.

They groaned, they stirred, they all uprose,
Nor spake, nor moved their eyes;
It had been strange, even in a dream,
To have seen those dead men rise.

The mariner was rescued when the ship reached his home, and the tattered ship sank into the ocean. As part of his penance and a second chance at life, the mariner now wanders from town to town looking for people who need to hear his message, giving those who hear it an opportunity to change their ways without going through an ordeal of their own. The message is to value all life in its many and varied forms.

Farewell, farewell! But this I tell
To thee, thou Wedding Guest!
He prayeth well, who loveth well
Both man and bird and beast.
He prayeth best, who loveth best
All things great and small;
For the dear God who loveth us,
He made and loveth all.

> **ON THE WWMDFK? WEBSITE:**
>
> *Rather than hard tack or salted fish, we thought you might enjoy some wedding punch so you can celebrate along with the mariner*

— Dianne

ANCIENT MARINER WATCH CAP
Designed by Dianne Read–Jackson

A watch cap is a close fitting hat that sailors wear to keep their heads warm in cold weather when it is their turn to be "on watch." The first recorded use of the term watch cap is from 1835 and the caps were originally knit in Navy Blue. I have knit this cap in grey and black to suit the mood of the poem. It is for those times when —

The ice was here, the ice was there,
The ice was all around:
It cracked and growled, and roared and howled,
Like noises in a swound!

You will want to knit one for your favorite mariner or landlubber to keep their head and ears toasty warm.

Egalité

SIZE
One size fits most

FINISHED MEASUREMENTS
Circumference: 18in [46cm] unstretched

MATERIALS
- [MC] Drops Karisma Superwash Wool [100% superwash wool; 115yds/105m per 50g skein; 10 WPI], 2 skeins #21 gray
- [CC] Drops Karisma Superwash Wool, 1 skein #53 black

Set of four or five US 4 [3.5mm] double pointed needles
 Stitch markers

GAUGE
24 sts = 4in [10cm] in 3x2 Rib, measured unstretched

PATTERN NOTES
This hat is knit in the round and should be cast on using a stretchy cast on method. I used the knitted cast on, the cable cast on will also work well.[4]

STITCH GUIDE
3x2 Rib (multiple of 5 sts)
Rnd 1: *K3, p2; rep from * to end.
Rep Rnd 1.

PATTERN
With MC, cast on 110 sts. Divide evenly over 3 or 4 needles and join to work in the round, taking care not to twist. Work 7 rnds 3x2 Rib.
Change to CC. Knit 1 rnd. Work 4 rnds 3x2 Rib.
Change to MC. Knit 1 rnd. Work 6 rnds 3x2 Rib.
Change to CC. Knit 1 rnd. Work 4 rnds 3x2 Rib.
Change to MC. Knit 1 rnd. Work in 3x2 Rib
until hat measures 8.5in [21.5cm] from cast on.

Crown Decreases
Rnd 1: *K1, k2tog, p2; rep from * to end. 88 sts.
Rnd 2: *K2, p2; rep from * to end.
Rnd 3: *K2, p2tog; rep from * to end. 66 sts.
Rnd 4: *K2, p1; rep from * to end.
Rnd 5: *K2tog, p1; rep from * to end. 44 sts.
Rnd 6: *K1, p1; rep from * to end.
Rnds 7 and 8: *K2tog; rep from * around. 11 sts.

Finishing
Using a tapestry needle, thread the yarn through the remaining stitches as you take them off the knitting needles and pull all stitches tight. Plunge needle through the center of the circle formed by these stitches and give another tug to make sure all of the stitches are pulled together tightly. Weave the end in securely on the inside of the hat.

IMPROVE YOUR STRIPES:

Here is a great tip I learned from Meg Swanson for sharp, clean stripes. Work the first round in your new color completely in knit stitch all the way around. This avoids the color blips on the purl stitches of your ribbing. Then continue your following rows in your established ribbing pattern and the ribbing will still be corrugated as if all of the stitches were worked in the ribbing stitches.

---

4 — http://www.youtube.com/watch?v=e4p6ybqnvVc

Winged Monkey Minions

INTERLUDE III

The Wonderful Wizard of Oz— L. Frank Baum
Illustrated by W. W. Denslow

I would not describe myself as a particularly fearful child, aside from the usual pantheon of under–the–bed–and–in–the–closet boogeymen, but I possessed an unusually robust number of scary media moments indelibly burned into my psyche. (Bear with me here, I'm a child of the '70s, and as such the miracles that were television and film played a crucial role in my formative years. We'll get to the lit soon, I promise.) As a result, I find myself gifted with an array of totally irrational visceral reactions that leave me with heart racing and palms sweating at the thought of things such as Sleestak (I still hear that horrid hissing in my dreams), The Bumble Snow Monster of the North ("doll–mation"… even the word makes me shudder), Ricardo Montalban (keep your crazy *Star Trek* ear bugs to yourself, please!), the animated version of Gollum (I so did not need a visual for this one)…and Flying Monkeys.

I can't remember the first time I saw the film. It seems like it was always around—the movie every kid was supposed to love. Not me. How I dreaded *The Wizard of Oz* popping up in the prime time line–up or ambushing me in that safest of all media–blackout refuges: school. Packs of lurking, bell–hop clad Technicolor gray monkeys eclipsed every bit of glitz on those ruby slippers, soured every note of every song and made me want to bop Glinda over the head with her very own sparkly wand before she could set Dorothy on that yellow–bricked path to certain furry ambush.

So, I grew up hating *The Wizard of Oz*, thinking with deep–seated dread of the next time I would be persecuted by viewing it and resisting all attempts made to get me to read *The Wonderful Wizard of Oz*. In my head, if the movie was that freaky, the book must be so, so, so very much worse. The plan to keep it firmly off my reading list proceeded swimmingly until well into adulthood when I stumbled across Gregory Maguire's *Wicked*, which I had trouble following as it is very much not based on the movie alone. Interest piqued, I headed for the library and then obsessively read each and every Oz book Mr. Baum wrote.

I will admit to a hefty dose of dread when I sat down with that first volume. "Here be monsters" may as well have been branded into the cover. Imagine my surprise when I found this front and center:

Introduction

Folk lore, legends, myths and fairy tales have followed childhood through the ages, for every healthy youngster has a wholesome and instinctive love for stories fantastic, marvelous and manifestly unreal. The winged fairies of Grimm and Andersen have brought more happiness to childish hearts than all other human creations.

Yet the old–time fairy tale, having served for generations, may now be classed as "historical" in the children's library; for the time has come for a series of newer "wonder tales" in which the stereotyped genie, dwarf and fairy are eliminated, together with all the horrible and blood–curdling incidents devised by their authors to point a fearsome moral to each tale. Modern education includes morality; therefore the modern child seeks only entertainment in its wonder-tales and gladly dispenses with all disagreeable incident. Having this thought in mind, the story of The Wizard of Oz *was written solely to pleasure children of to–day. It aspires to being a modernized fairy tale, in which the wonderment and joy are retained and the heart–aches and nightmares are left out.*

L. Frank Baum
Chicago, April, 1900.

     Really, I think there was an audible "clunk" as something immutably shifted in my brain. While as a parent I can definitely shoot about a thousand holes in his logic concerning the teaching of morality and, after reading the books, am always prepared to point out their own hefty share of "disagreeable incident," I was in that moment totally charmed. The fairy tale devotee in me most definitely perked up, though more than a bit of suspicion remained. How to reconcile crazed flying monkey attacks with this intent? With each page however, it became increasingly clear just how successful he was. This is a feat of amazingly gentle storytelling. Nothing really fazes Dorothy as she moves through this world of strange yet wondrous beings, places, and events. Oh sure, she sheds a few tears, but generally out of frustration, rather from the fright of, say, meeting a talking scarecrow who takes to following her about. The story unfolds in simply–told, matter–of–fact events peppered with delightfully practical bits that evoke what a child would in fact be doing in that circumstance. One of my favorites being this passage after the Wicked Witch of the West has been vanquished:

Dorothy went to the Witch's cupboard to fill her basket with food for the journey, and there she saw the Golden Cap. She tried it on her own head and found that it fitted her exactly. She did not know anything about the charm of the Golden Cap, but she saw that it was pretty, so she made up her mind to wear it and carry her sun–bonnet in the basket.

Because who wouldn't be thinking of food after melting a wicked witch and thus liberating an entire people from enslavement… and then finding a pretty hat? SCORE!

But still, the monkeys, right? No doubt about it, Winged Monkeys tear the scarecrow to bits, batter the tin woodsman and bind the lion, serving as the last of a series of admittedly rather lame attacks waged by the Wicked Witch. They do however have a sob story, a mitigating factor in their favor, if you will. I'm a hopeless champion of the underdog and this totally redeemed their literary selves in my eyes. They've always been a mischievous lot it seems, and at one point they dumped a powerful princess' intended in a river for a joke and ruined his silky, velvety finery. In punishment, they are forever bound to fulfill three wishes of the wearer of the Golden Cap—current owner being said Witch. It's all very simply told. The movie images are dripping with an intensity that is—with crystal clear intent—not in the written words. A monkey's gotta do what a monkey's gotta do. End of story and off they go.

Adult me can now sit back sipping a comforting cup of awe and appreciate the evil genius it took to corrupt the simple, childlike grace Baum presents. I totally understand why it happened. Moral conflict drives a story and provides the reader with opportunity to identify with the characters and revel in the outcome. That doesn't mean I have to like it.

So, I move through my adult life still assiduously avoiding the movie while pushing the books on friend and foe alike while I wait for my own children to be able to devour them as their very own special treats… and when asked "what would Madame Defarge knit?" Well, in the Land of Oz, I have no doubt it would be monkeys.

—Dawn

WINGED MONKEY MINIONS
Designed by Dawn Ellerd

Packs of mischievous and misunderstood flying monkeys, I can handle. Legions of flying monkeys bent on world domination by an evil puppet master, I cannot. Either way, you can now make your own. My versions wear Golden Caps. If you choose the dark road of enslavement, you're on your own as to designing headwear, because in this instance I firmly believe that what Madame Defarge would knit involves simian liberation.

FINISHED MEASUREMENTS
Approx. 8in [20.5cm] tall

Égalité

MATERIALS
- [MC] Lion Brand Nature's Choice Organic Cotton [100% cotton; 103 yd/94m per 83g skein; 8 WPI], 1 skein #125 Walnut
- [CC1] Lion Brand Nature's Choice Organic Cotton, 1 skein #098 Almond
- [CC2] Lion Brand Cotton Ease [50% cotton/50% acrylic; 207 yd/189m per 100g skein; 9 WPI], 1 skein #186 Maize
- US H [5mm] crochet hook
- Two Creatology 18mm Animal Eyes
- Polyester stuffing material, or the stuffing of your choice
- Weighted beads (recommended, but optional)
- Ten size 6/0 seed beads, red

GAUGE
Not important for this pattern

PATTERN NOTES

➤ Weighted beads are not strictly necessary, but if you like your creations to stand up, they are very helpful (and sanitary if you have concerns about little visitors or perhaps dogs that hunt down stuffies to munch on, having smelled rice or millet or some other goodie inside).

➤ When crocheting with pre-strung beads, simply snug the bead up against the last stitch worked and proceed. The bead will pop into place.

➤ The monkey is worked from the bottom up, stuffing as you go. The hat is worked separately, then slip-stitched onto the head opening. Wings and ears are worked separately and sewn on.

➤ For foundation single crochet (fsc), see Glossary, page 192.

➤ Where pattern directs you to join, work a sl st in first sc unless otherwise specified.

PATTERN BEGINS

Body

Rnd 1: With MC, ch2, sc8 in second ch from hook. Join.
Rnd 2: Ch1. Sc in first st, sc2 in each st around. Sc in first st. Join. 16 sc.
Rnd 3: Ch1. Sc in first st, *sc, sc2; repeat from * around. Sc in first st. Join. 25 sc.
Rnds 4-5: Ch1. Sc around. Join.
Rnd 6: Ch1. Sc in first st, *sc, sc, sc2; repeat from * around. Sc in first st. Join. 34 sc.
Rnds 7-9: Ch1. Sc around. Join.
Rnd 10: Ch1. Skip first st, *sc, sc, sc2tog; repeat from * to last st. Sc2tog last st and first st. Join. 25 sc.
Rnds 11-12: Ch1. Sc around. Join.
Rnd 13: Ch1. Skip first st, *sc2tog, sc; repeat from * to last st. Sc2tog last st and first st. Join. 16 sc.

Fill the bottom third of the body with beads and stuff the rest of the body firmly full before continuing with the head.

Rnd 14: Ch1. Sc blo in first st, sc2 blo in each st around. Sc blo in first st. Join. 32 sc.
Rnds 15-19: Ch1. Sc around. Join.
Rnd 20: Ch1. Skip first st, *sc2tog, sc; repeat from * to last st. Sc2tog last st and first st. Join. 19 sc. Break yarn, tie off, weave in ends.

Place eyes. Make ears and wings and sew on.

Ears (make 2)
Row 1: With CC1, ch2, sc6 in second ch from hook. Finish last st (last yo and pull through 2 loops on hook) with MC. Break CC1.
Row 2: With MC, turn, sl st across. Break yarn leaving long end for sewing. Tie off.
Wings (make 2)
Row 1: With CC1, ch4 (counts as 1ch + 1dc), dc7 in fourth ch from hook. 8 dc.
Row 2: Ch3 (counts as 1dc), turn. Dc at base of turning ch, dc2 in each st across. 16 dc.

Row 3: Ch3 (counts as 1dc), turn. Dc at base of turning ch, *dc, dc2; repeat from * to last 2 sts, dc in next st, dc6 in last st. 30 dc.
Row 4: Turning to work along straight edge of half-circle: Sl st in base of Row 2. Dc6 in center st. Sl st in base of Row 2. Dc5 at base of first st of Row 3. Sl st at top of turning ch. Break yarn, leaving a 18in [45.5cm] long tail for one of the wings and a short tail for the other. Tie off.

To join wings together: Hold wings front sides facing and at one end, using the long tail, sl st tog 5 sts picking up one loop from each wing. Tie off. Sew wings on the back, at top of body, below juncture with head.

Stuff head before proceeding with hat.

Hat
String 10 seed beads on CC2.
Rnd 1: With CC2, fsc30. Join.
Rnd 2: Ch1. Sc around. Join.
Rnd 3: Ch1. Sc blo around, slipping bead before each 6th st, making sure it pops to the front of the work. Join.
Rnd 4: Ch1. Sc in next 3 sts, slip bead before next st, then continue in sc slipping bead before every 6th st. Join.
Rnd 5: Ch1. Sl blo around. Join.
Rnd 6: Ch1. Sc around. Join.
Rnd 7: Ch1. *Sc in next 3 sts, sc2tog; repeat from * around. Join. 24 sts.
Rnds 8, 10, 12, 14, 16: Ch1. Sc around. Join.
Rnd 9: Ch1. *Sc, sc, sc2tog; repeat from * around. Join. 18 sts.
Rnd 11: Ch1. *Sc, sc2tog; repeat from * around. Join. 12 sts.
Rnd 13: Ch1. *Sc2tog; repeat from * to last st, sc. Join. 6 sts.
Rnd 15: Ch1. *Sc2tog; repeat from * around. Join. 3 sts.

Break yarn. Tie off, weave in ends. With yarn held double, join at Rnd 1 and sc flo around brim. Join. Break yarn, leaving enough yarn to sew hat to head. Do that and you are done. (Note that hat is not stuffed so that you can flop over the tip.)

ON THE WWMDIK? WEBSITE:

Feeling the need for a potassium infusion to buck up your strength before fighting evil? Perhaps some Banana Bundt Cake or a Banana Shake?

WOMEN OF VALOR

Eshet Chayil is a twenty–two verse poem with which King Solomon concludes the book of Proverbs.

Eshet chayil mi yimtza v'rachok mip'ninim michrah
Batach bah lev ba'lah v'shalal lo yechsar
—Proverbs 31: 10

Awoman of valor, who can find her? for her price is far above rubies... I found a wonderful blog post by Sandy Hovatter dissecting the word "chayil" and its use in the Tanach and found, among other things, that some women shudder at this passage. They've been taught that a "Proverbs 31 Woman" is some unattainable ideal of virtuous and pure womanhood. A quick look at the blog post (or an equally quick read here) makes it rather clear that "a woman of valor" was exactly the kind of "tough chick" that you would have needed to be back in Solomon's day.

According to Ms. Hovatter's blog, the word "chayil" is translated in other parts of Biblical texts as: army, strength, power, and worth (to name a few). This word, "chayil," is not a word to describe a submissive woman who shrinks back from challenges. This woman rises ready to seize the day, take some names, and kick some *tuchis*.

After she analyzed the Biblical uses of the word, Hovatter re–translated the passage thusly:

> *A powerful woman, a woman of valor is more precious than rubies. A woman of strength, who can find her?*

That seems closer to the women we admire in literature, no? It's also interesting that these lines were supposed to be said to Solomon by his mother—advice on ruling a kingdom and finding a nice, strong girl to settle down with. Can you not just hear Solomon's mom saying to her Mah Jong buddies, "eh, she's all right, but is she good enough for my son the king?" Puts a different spin on it when you know it's a mother talking to her son!

Nonetheless, if you look at the laundry list of what a woman is expected to do, these stand out to me:

13 She seeketh wool, and flax, and worketh willingly with her hands...
19 She layeth her hands to the spindle, and her hands hold the distaff...
22 She maketh herself coverings of tapestry; her clothing is silk and purple...
24 She maketh fine linen, and selleth it; and delivereth girdles unto the merchant.

25 Strength and honor are her clothing; and she shall rejoice in time to come...
27 She looketh well to the ways of her household, and eateth not the bread of idleness...
31 Give her of the fruit of her hands;

She's a fiber artist! Among other things... among many, many other things...

My husband was looking at this passage with me (and generously, did not attempt to compare me to the description) and pointed out that from Eve to Deborah to Esther, Biblical women were tough. They were valorous—in any sense of the word. He also pointed out, as Irina Dunn did (and Gloria Steinem popularized and Bono sang), that "a woman needs a man, like a fish needs a bicycle," especially if the woman in question lived up to the complete list presented in Proverbs 31. Good grief, if she had all those qualities, *she* would be the king.

But...

I spent my childhood trying to be a "good girl," as many of us did. I still do my best to be "good," though I'm sure I've inadvertently offended by not knowing what to say, sticking both feet in my mouth (I'm quite limber) while stammering or trying to bridge a silence with humor. But I always make those mistakes while trying to keep others at their ease— or at least laughing. I'm not really in the strident "say it loud, say it proud, and damn those who disagree" camp. At heart, I would still rather resemble Marmee than the Good Madame.

But I don't.

I have my bouts of anger, dreams of retribution for real or imagined slights, fits of pique (I love the word, though not the state of mind so much), just like anyone does. Not very Marmee–like, is it?

I'm slowly making my peace with that—and thank goodness because, Lord knows, I'm not getting any younger. But I still look at the women represented in this section of our book and I wonder... in their place, in their time, with their challenges, would Marmee have done any differently? If her family had been harmed or her girls threatened, would she have gone the way of the Madame? Those musings lead me back to critical self–examination. Would I be as strong or as brave as they are in their situations?

I like to hope I would have been. I've had my moments of small valor—giving birth, ushering students out of the path of the 9/11 attacks, driving 25 miles on ice–covered mountain switchbacks to get our family home safely—but those moments aren't things that haven't been done before, or by others, or better. As scary as 9/11 was for us, I wasn't the first teacher to get kids out of a bad situation and my life wasn't ever really in the danger the tower workers were in (my lungs maybe, but that's another essay). I gave birth to my sons in sterile environments with clean water and great midwives. As dramatic as childbirth is, mine weren't traumatic. I've been lucky and life has been relatively easy, so why is it that women of valor attract me so? The chances of me running up against a wolf, or a revolution, or a vampire, or the Athenian and Spartan armies are astronomically slim. And I'd be a fool to think my life would be better if I left my husband and children like Nora. They are my life. So what is it about these ladies that I connect with?

I think, perhaps, it's the side of me that wants to be Dorothy Parker, to say what I think without reservation or apology, to offend who I offend and not care, because if those who feel slighted were just a little smarter, or a little quicker, they would have come back with something even better that I would respect. I like to think I might have been a heckuva revolutionary.

In another life.
In another time.

But for now, with my home and my kids and my husband, I think I'll settle for making things that keep them warm and that remind them, every time they wear their Tardis socks, that their mother loves them more than rubies.

In this section of the book you will find patterns that give you a new look at Little Red's riding hood, glacial gauntlets to reflect Nora's surprisingly icy strength, a blood red shawl for Mina to wear when searching for Lucy in Dracula's graveyards, a scarlet cowl worthy of Hester's incandescent beauty, a wine-red stole with hidden messages from the Good Madame, Jane Fairfax's tippet, and a revolutionary's chiton. Strong women. Valorous characters. May we all find their strength in us when we most need it.

Wolf-Slayer

LITTLE RED RIDING HOOD
The Brothers Grimm

You know the story. Darling child traipsing through the wood, taking a basket of goodies to ailing Grandmother, is led astray by Big Bad Wolf, who then dines on Granny and Little Red before succumbing to woodsman's axe. Granny and Little Red miraculously emerge whole and unharmed from the wolf's stomach and all live happily ever after. Nice.

Yet curiously unfulfilling. The exact feeling most of our modernized, Westernized, sanitary fairy tales left me with as a child: B.O.R.E.D.

Until I hit Brit Lit class in high school and finally had a teacher who thought we were capable of handling the real deal. Beowulf (all 3182 fabulously alliterative lines of it), The Canterbury Tales (yes, even the ribald ones), and more original Welsh, Celtic, Irish and Scottish folk tales than I could shake my Walkman at.

Huzzah! All of a sudden, "happily" did not necessarily describe the state of ever after. Not all princesses were vapid and incapable of taking care of themselves. Not all kisses had transformative powers. Sometimes the bad guys won and the good guys lost. Finally, a world full of wonder, where anything could — and did — happen to anyone, revealing the depth of its shadow. Rationality and logic may not have ruled, but neither did sentimentality and virtue.

The few stories we read and analyzed in class served as my gateway drug. One led to another to another. English led to French led to German led to Italian led to Greek and on and on and on. Tales and fables and myths, oh my!

Folk stories are like one giant, immensely fascinating, interconnected web. Or maybe a jigsaw puzzle. Or better yet, a set of tangrams. You've seen them, right? Those sets of tiles that you combine and recombine to make various shapes and pictures. As with fables, the basic elements remain the same but combine in unique patterns to reveal a larger whole. Princes. Princesses. Children lost in woods or down wells. Enchanted frogs, pigs and poultry. Wicked witches, wolves and wives. Some are good. A few are bad. Most are both.

Good stuff.

Undeniably, my favorites would be the tales laid down by Jacob and Wilhelm Grimm, perhaps because they were the foundation for so many of our most iconic modern fairy stories…but oh so much better. The Frog Prince. Cinderella. Sleeping Beauty. Rapunzel. Hansel and Gretel. Tom Thumb. Rumplestiltskin. Snow White. They're all here, and so is Little Red Riding Hood.

Actually, a better translation for the original German appears to be "Little Red Cap." No matter. She's still tasked with taking goodies through the woods to Grandmother's house. She's still waylaid by a conniving, charming wolf who eats her grandmother before Red can make the scene, and who, when she eventually does show up, snaps her up as well.

Here's where I have my first moment. In the original, when Little Red walks in Granny's strangely open cottage door, "she had such a strange feeling that she said to herself, 'Oh dear! How uneasy I feel to–day, and at other times I like being with grandmother so much.' " HA! Do you see that? Intuition! Here is this story, with roots in the 14th century, and part of the moral is to actually get girls to trust their gut. Sweet!

So, the story proceeds apace. Woodsman manages to slice open the wolf without killing him, Red and Granny do indeed pop out unscathed, but for some reason Red decides to sew stones in the wolf's stomach to kill him. A little perplexed by the wolf dispatching technique employed? Perhaps that's why the mutations I grew up with as a child had the wolf being handily carved up by the woodsman. While I appreciate the Grimm Brothers' apparent desire to have Red save herself I just cannot bend my brain around this one. You've just popped out of the gullet of a devious stalker and you decide to run for some stones? To sew into his stomach? Couldn't she just have bashed him over the head and been done with it? I suppose that's not very lady–like, but is torture really more seemly? Though hey, as I've never been in that position, who am I to critique, eh?

Now, in any version I heard growing up, this pretty much ended the story. In the Grimms' version, there's more. Little Red shows she has learned her lesson next time she is tasked with traveling to Granny's. Giving a new wolf the cold shoulder, she dashes ahead to the cottage where she and Granny lay a trap for this wolf, and our furry friend ends up drowning in sausage water. Ugh.

But notice: No woodsman. No prince. No magical powers or enchanted shoes. Just the materials to hand and their own wits. It appears Red and Granny may even be having some fun.

In my mind, Granny and Little Red eclipse the Wonder Twins for super powers. Invulnerability, intuition, inventive wit, and sausage making skills — what more can you ask for in heroines? One could most definitely do worse. I like to think of them as the matriarchs of a secret underground society. Long live the wolf–slayers!

— Dawn

WOLF–SLAYER
Designed by Dawn Ellerd

A shocking red hood may not be inconspicuous enough for our good Madame, but I cannot imagine a better homage to the dynamic duo of Grandmother and daughter…and no worries for giving oneself away with unsightly blood stains. Happy hunting.

SIZE
One size fits most

FINISHED MEASUREMENTS
Hood: 12.5in [31.5cm] tall, 15in [38cm] deep
Scarf: 4in [10cm] wide, 70in [178cm] long

Egalité

Materials
- Briar Rose Fibers Robusta [100% wool; 500yd/457m per 454g skein; 7 WPI], 1 skein (please note: this yarn is dyed in one of a kind lots, and there is no color name)
- US L [8mm] crochet hook
- Fifteen 10mm metal beads

GAUGE
12 sts and 9 rows = 4in [10cm] in counterpane pattern

STITCH GUIDE
Counterpane Pattern (any number of sts)
Row 1: Ch1, turn. Sc in each st across.
Row 2: Ch2, turn. [Yo, insert hook, draw up loop and continue through first loop on hook, yo, draw through rem 2 loops] in each st across.
Rep Rows 1-2.

Puff Stitch: [yo, insert hook, draw up loop] three times, yo, draw through all loops on hook.

PATTERN NOTES
For foundation single crochet (fsc), see Glossary, page 192.

PATTERN BEGINS
Hood
Hood is worked flat in one piece, then folded and seamed up the back.
Row 1: Leaving a 10in [25cm] tail, fsc53.
Row 2: Ch1, turn. *Sc, ch1, skip next st; rep from * to last st, sc in last st.
Row 3: Ch2, turn. *Puff st in ch1-sp, ch1, skip 1 sc; repeat from * to last st, dc in last st.
Row 4: Rep Row 2.
Rows 5-34: Work in counterpane pattern.

Fold rectangle in half crosswise. Seam the two halves of the long edge together with sl st: align the edge sts tog and insert hook through one loop from each adjacent st for a neat, decorative seam. Break yarn leaving a 10in [25cm] tail. This is the point of your hood. The seam runs down the back.

Scarf

Row 1: Leaving a 10in [25cm] tail, ch50. Sl st in each row along bottom edge of hood, in what were the edge sts of the original rectangle. When you reach the last st, ch51. 135 sts.
Row 2: Ch1, turn. Sc blo in each st across, being careful not to twist the chains where they meet the body of the hood.
Rows 3-5: Work same as Rows 2-4 of Hood.
Row 6: Ch1, turn. Sc across.
Rows 7-9: Work same as Rows 2-4 of Hood.
Row 10: Ch1, turn. Sc across. Break yarn leaving a 10in [25cm] tail, tie off.

Tassels

1. Cut thirty 20in [51cm] strands of yarn. Separate into five bundles of six strands each
2. At each corner of the scarf, insert a bundle, pulling it halfway through, then doubling it over. You now have twelve strands held together.
3. Divide them into three groups of four strands each (except at the corners with the long tails — incorporate your tail into one of the groups and save weaving in ends!) and braid for 2in [5cm].
4. Holding all 12 strands together again, make a loop and pull the ends through, knotting it off.
5. Again divide into three groups. String one bead over each group and knot it off.

Repeat at all four scarf corners and at the peak of the hood.

ON THE **WWMDFK?** WEBSITE:

Feeling the need for a basket of goodies? You'll find lots of ideas in our Wolf Slayer picnic food fun guide.

Nora's Glacial Gauntlets

A DOLL'S HOUSE
Henrik Ibsen

SPOILER ALERT—END OF PLAY DISCUSSED IN ESSAY

Poor Nora.

I first read Ibsen at university, but we read *Ghosts*, not *A Doll's House*. I was largely unmoved by Ibsen back then. To be sure, I could appreciate the writing (or the translation) and I found the conflict fascinating (the sins of the father visited on the son) but it was kind of a "guy play" as far as I was concerned.

Later, I read *A Doll's House*.

Eh.

This is why I love hosting CraftLit. I receive email all the time saying what I'm about to write here: It was better the second time…when I was a little older. When I knew more.

In the late 1990s, my husband and I were lucky enough to see Janet McTeer in a new version of *A Doll's House*. If you've never been lucky enough to see Ms. McTeer on stage, let me give you some context.

She's tall.
Super tall.
And a blazing redhead.
And amazing.
She is no wee, wimpy Nora Helmer, is what I'm trying to say.

The way we understood Ibsen's story in school was that poor fluff–headed Nora was married to an older Torvald. It was a little creepy, honestly, what with him always calling her his little bird and all, and when she left at the end I think we all thought, "Well, duh. Yeah. I mean, who'd want to stick around that boring old coot?"

Then we saw McTeer. And Torvald, played by Owen Teale, was a revelation. He was young. And hot. And suddenly everything about this play changed.

Now Nora, who is giddy and childish at the outset, is also an imposing figure. It's all the more disturbing to see someone so physically present be treated like a little, weak doll— and enjoy it. Her husband, whom she will leave by play's end, is an attractive man and they are quite obviously drawn to each other. And although there is love there, there is also the constant patronization of Nora.

By the end of the play, when Nora's whole world has fallen apart, she is left with a choice.

She has a husband who loves her, two children, and a nice—if shakily financed—life. Nonetheless, she chooses to leave the doll's house she's been living in. When the door closes and the lock clicks, the finality of her choice echoes throughout the theater. When done well, it is impossible not to weep for the unfairness of it all.

During the course of the play, Nora has grown up, and grown strong—strong as a glacier. She moves slowly but inexorably towards her final decision, and like a glacier, she sweeps everything away in front of her and with her, off a cliff into the unknown.

I was lucky enough to meet a glacier in person. Far above the Contiguous 48, beyond a cold, grey stretch of choppy ocean, there lies a calm, steely stretch of bay bound by glacial elegance. The Hubbard Glacier calved the whole time our ship sat in the bay. It was an awesome sight, in the true sense of the word. Really *seeing* natural magnificence is generally not an everyday occurrence. Even living by the Hudson it became commonplace to see the spectacular Palisades across the river. Easy to just look and nod without seeing the beauty and raw power that's always present in nature. My little cruise party—many of whom are designers in this book—all agreed that we should find some way to memorialize the majesty of the moment and location.

In an attempt to recapture a very small piece of that magnificent sight, the pattern you have here uses yarns hand–dyed to represent the many colors visible in the glacial icebergs that meandered by us on their lazy way back down the channel. It is my small attempt to capture the complexity of a glacial environment—and a reflection of how complex a character Nora can be.

The gauntlet's physical purpose is to bridge the inevitable gap between coat and hand on those blustery days when a sweater, coat, and scarf are simply not enough and one's mittens are woefully brief in the wrist area. The color design is meant to give the wearer two choices: light side out or dark side out, depending on what you are wearing.

Ten colors appear in the gauntlet—five different blues—modeled on the "Blue Shimmer" pattern from the Bohus studios. Adjustments have been made to alter the original yoke pattern and make it a cylinder, so you will have some rows that have special notes. But the design is largely the same; only the colors have changed.

Instructions for dyeing these colors using Permanent Protein Dye Disguised as Children's Drink (*think Kool Aid*) follow the pattern, and photos of the process are available at the website.

— Heather

NORA'S GLACIAL GAUNTLETS
Designed by Heather Anne Ordover

The Bohus Studio is famous for its intricate patterning for good reason. As this gauntlet grows you will find the subtle difference in blues to be quite lovely. The occasional splash of red mirrors both the rust color that appears in some icebergs and the temper of Nora that finally flared at the end of the play.

Consider weaving in or otherwise trapping your ends as you knit. You will save yourself quite a lot of stitching work (not to mention annoyance) at the end.

SIZE
One size fits most women

FINISHED MEASUREMENTS
Circumference: 8in [20.5cm]
Length: 6.5in [16.5cm] (possibly longer after whapping, see Notes)

Egalité

MATERIALS
- Knit Picks Bare Stroll Fingering Sock [75% superwash wool, 25% nylon; 462 yd/423m per 100g skein; 14 WPI], 1 hank re-skeined into smaller (10g) hanks for dyeing.
- Set of four or five US 3 [3.25mm] double pointed needles
- Stitch marker

GAUGE
28 sts and 30 rows = 4in [10cm] in stockinette with stranded colorwork

PATTERN NOTES
I found that the Bohus design, with its intermittent purl stitches, bunched up while on the needles. However, Bohus knitting was often done with angora blends, so to try to make my piece a little fluffier, I soaked it and whapped it a few times against a tile counter. This particular yarn didn't fluff up much, but it sure brought the pattern out and improved the overall look. Don't fear the whap!

PATTERN BEGINS
With main neutral color, cast on 56, divide over three or four needles, pm and join to work in the round. Work in p2, k2 rib for 5 rnds.
Work Rnds 1-39 of Chart. The outlined box shows the pattern repeat. Don't be alarmed that the repeat seems to jump around; just follow along and it will come out all right.
Work 5 rnds p2, k2 rib.
Bind off in rib. Weave in ends, if you haven't knitted them in along the way. Wet, whap, and dry.

■ Prussian blue

☐ Neutral

% Kingfisher blue

Spectrum blue

◆ Emerald green

▨ No stitch

◥ Ochre

> Mineral green

△ Copper beech

+ Blue-gray

⌒ Vermilion

If a stitch has a white background, it is knit.
If a stitch has a gray background, it is purled.

DYEING

Begin by assembling the troops: Distilled white vinegar, mason jars, a large soup pot (or turkey roaster or any large pan – the dye won't be touching the pot, so it doesn't matter if it's reactive or not), kettle, small skeins of yarn, permanent-acid-dye-masquerading-as-a-children's-drink, craft sticks, coffee filters (to test color), manila tie-tags for keeping track of skeins (super important).

Once you have all the pieces, you may begin the process.

- Boil water in kettle while heating a few inches of water in the soup pot.
- Place mason jars (heat-resistant jars) into the water and fill them with 1/4 cup or so of vinegar (it is not an exact science – acidic is acidic. You can't make the dye more acidic by adding more vinegar, as the pH is a fixed number). Once the vinegar has started warming up, add your powdered drink mix. Recipes used in this pattern were:

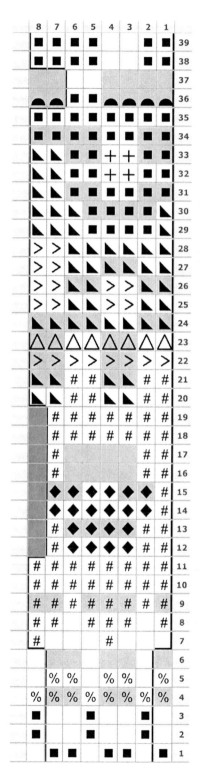

- MINERAL GREEN: 2 lemon-lime (green)+ 1/3 grape (1½ hours to exhaust)
- EMERALD GREEN: 2 lemon-lime (green) (1½ hours to exhaust)
- PRUSSIAN BLUE: 5 berry blue (1½ hours to exhaust)
- VERMILION: 1 cherry + 1 strawberry + 1/3 grape (1½ hours to exhaust)
- BLUE-GREY: 1 berry blue + 1/3 grape (1-1/2 hours to exhaust)
- COPPER BEECH: ½ orange + ½ grape (1-1/2 hours to exhaust)
- KINGFISHER BLUE: 1 berry blue (20 minutes)
- SPECTRUM: 3 berry blue (30 minutes)
- OCHRE: 3 bags Earl Grey tea (1-1/2 hours to exhaust)

Stir until powder is completely blended using a different stick for each jar. Stir in boiling water to top. Test color by dripping a drop or two off a stirring stick onto a coffee filter.

Gently add skeins to the water and set a timer or note the clock time. The lighter blue colors have different times indicated than the rest of the colors. Once you've removed and rinsed the lighter blues (they will not have exhausted their dye) you can walk away, leaving the heat on very low. Within an hour and a half, all dye should be exhausted, meaning the water in the jars will be clear (ish). When the water is clear enough to see through, there's little chance of the fiber getting darker so you may as well take it out. Coffee makes a lovely dye, as does tea.

FOR MORE ON DYEING:

If you would like to see the basic colors available there are two tutorials that were used in the blending of the colors seen in this pattern. One is by Kristi Porter at Knitty.com and one at The Piper by Barbara M. Harris-Pruitt.

THE SCARLET LETTER
Nathaniel Hawthorne

Her attire, which, indeed, she had wrought for the occasion, in prison, and had modeled much after her own fancy, seemed to express the attitude of her spirit, the desperate recklessness of her mood, by its wild and picturesque peculiarity... On the breast of her gown, in fine red cloth, surrounded with an elaborate embroidery and fantastic flourishes of gold thread, appeared the letter A. It was so artistically done, and with so much fertility and gorgeous luxuriance of fancy, that it had all the effect of a last and fitting decoration to the apparel which she wore; and which was of a splendor in accordance with the taste of the age, but greatly beyond what was allowed by the sumptuary regulations of the colony.

The Scarlet Letter, Chapter Two, "The Market–Place"

I first read *The Scarlet Letter* in high school, a small, academic girls' school in an old and conservative New England industrial city. This was "back in the day" and I am not sure that my classmates and I understood exactly what Hester had done. Okay, we weren't that naïve. We knew she had the baby and kept it, which would have been almost unheard of even three hundred years later at the time we were reading. But, as I recall, the focus of our discussion was on symbolism and the counting of the many references to the letter A in the text, rather than on characterization, historical context, or anything connected to our own lives such as guilt, anger, revenge, jealousy, or love. Well, maybe guilt was brought up, as in "see how you will be punished if. . ." At any rate, as rambunctious, though properly uniformed, adolescent girls, we identified chiefly with Little Pearl, aka "The Elf Child," with her uncanny ability to say or do something outrageous in every circumstance. Her name became a code word for disrespect. "What would Little Pearl do?" indeed.

In Massachusetts, where I still live, the staples of tourism are, in addition to the Red Sox, literary figures, colonial architecture and artifacts, as well as Pilgrims, witches, pirates and ghosts. A revisit to the book was long overdue for me, and I was intrigued when the title was selected for the CraftLit podcast. What would I make of it now? Who was Hester? Was she a wimp, a ninny, a heroine, a harlot? Was Chillingworth as creepy as I remembered? And just what was up with Dimmesdale? Lover boy or lunkhead? What about Hawthorne's work? A long–winded bore or a page–turner?

As I listened, three things struck me: the gorgeous imagery, Hawthorne's sly humor, and the depth and complexity of his characters, particularly Hester. I was completely caught up in her situation and in awe of her dignity, her toughness, and her quiet refusal to play the groveling penitent while at the same time embracing all the pain of her punishment. In Hawthorne's view she's neither martyr nor Madonna, which leaves her— and us—in a very interesting position. Hester Prynne is a bit unusual when compared with other females depicted, or in some cases cartooned, by Hawthorne's contemporaries. We encounter her as an independent, adult person, with all the attendant contradictions and complexities, and we can look for ourselves in that jumble.

One element of Hester's character that I loved was what Hawthorne refers to as "all the combative energy of her character." Hmm–mm–mm, I think, maybe that's why I find her so interesting this time around. I remembered an acting class in which we had to name and describe our favorite actor —after which our teacher invited us to consider that what we had done was to describe some quality that was also ours. The exercise works for fiction as well. "Combative energy?" Anyone who knows me, knows that I have that in spades. I awarded bonus points to Hawthorne for having one of the gossips call Hester a "brazen hussy," because a teacher in my elementary school referred to certain (spirited and interesting) girls as "bold and brazen stumps."

Silliness aside, I kept wondering what I would have done in Hester's place. Run to the wilderness? Flee to another colony? Out Dimmesdale to the community? Poison Chillingworth and be done with it? Tough it out? I don't know the answer, but I love the questions, and I guess that's why the book is a classic.

As for inspiration, I like to think that, along with her daughter, it is Hester's creativity, her artful and intricate needlework, that allows her to keep on keepin' on. Her creations are not just a source of income, but a source of expression and satisfaction at a time in her sad life when everything else of comfort had been taken from her.

—Kathleen

MS PRYNNE
Designed by Kathleen Rogers

This neckwarmer is knit from the top down, first in the round, then switching to back and forth flat knitting, in a luxurious wool–silk fingering yarn held double. The woven cable pattern creates a fabric of undulating Scarlet Letter A's opening into a split yoke embellished with small beaded A's and a beaded border band, echoing Hester Prynne's extravagant and defiant embroidery. The open cables with their two limbs can also be seen to represent the duos in the book (Hester/Pearl, Dimmesdale/Chillingworth, Nature/Society Hester/Dimmesdale, and others).

There are several ways to wear this piece. The split yoke can be turned to the front or the back. The neck section can be turned under for a shorter ruff–like collar, or the yoke turned under for an ear–warmer. If you are feeling whimsical (be bold, like Little Pearl) the piece can be worn upside down on the head with the neck pulled down over the ears and the yoke sticking up like a crown.

At the end of the pattern, you will find "Variations on a Theme" which includes other Scarlet Letter inspired patterns that can be worked using the same stitches.

SIZE
One size fits all

Egalité

FINISHED MEASUREMENTS:
Lower edge circumference: 30in [76cm]
Upper edge circumference: 16.5in [42cm] (unstretched)
Length: 8.75in [22cm]

MATERIALS
- The March Hare Wool-Silk Fingering [70% merino wool, 30% silk; 435 yd/398m per 100g skein; 13 WPI], 1 skein color The Scarlet Letter

Note: As worked, the sample required 370yd/338m of fingering weight, held double; 185 yd/169m of worsted weight in a similar base yarn, held single, could be substituted.

- US 9 [5.5mm] circular needle, 16in or 24in [40cm or 60cm] long
- US 10 [6.5mm] circular needle, 16in [40cm] long
- Cable needle
- Stitch marker
- US H [5mm] crochet hook (optional, for edging yoke split)
- 123 seed beads size 6/0
- Steel crochet hook, US 7 [1.15 mm] (or size to fit beads) for placing beads

GAUGE

20 sts and 24 rows = 4in [10cm] in stockinette with smaller needles and two strands of yarn held together.

PATTERN NOTES

Piece is knit from the top down: in the round to the base of the neck, and then split and knit flat (back and forth) for the yoke. Yarn is held double throughout.

STITCH GUIDE

BUB (bring up bead): Slide pre-strung bead up yarn so that it sits directly next to st on needle, then work next st in pattern.

Place bead: Put bead on stitch using crochet hook (see beading help on page 145).

BDK (beaded dot knot stitch): Insert right-hand needle beneath the horizontal thread between the next two stitches on the left-hand needle and loosely draw up a loop (Loop A) of working yarn. Insert right needle again, this time above the same horizontal thread, and loosely draw up a loop (Loop B). For the moment, these loops sit on the right needle. Move working yarn to front of work. With small crochet hook, place bead on first stitch on left needle, then purl that stitch. Pass Loop A over Loop B and the purled stitch and off the needle, then pass Loop B over the purled stitch and off the needle.

C10L (or C12L): Place 5 (or 6) sts on cable needle and hold to front of work, k5 (or 6) sts, k5 (or 6) sts from cable needle

C10R (or C12R): Place 5 (or 6) sts on cable needle and hold to back of work, k5 (or 6) sts, k5 (or 6) sts from cable needle

PATTERN BEGINS

String 35 beads onto two strands of yarn held together, knotting the end. Measure out sufficient yarn for long-tail cast on, leaving the beads on the tail. With the larger needle and using the long-tail method, cast on 107 sts as foll: *Cast on 3, BUB; rep from * until 105 sts have been cast on and 35 beads have been used, cast on 2. 107 sts. Pm and join to work in the round.
Change to smaller needle.
Rnds 1-2: Knit.
Rnd 3: K1, C10L, *k5, C10L; rep from * to last 6 sts, k6.
Rnds 4-8: Knit.
Rnd 9: K6, C10R, *k5, C10R; rep from * to last st, k1.
Rnds 10-12: Knit.
Rnds 13-24: Rep Rnds 1-12.
Rnds 25-30: Rep Rnds 1-6.
Rnd 31 (inc rnd): K6, m1, *k5, m1; rep from * to last st, k1. 128 sts.
Rnds 32-33: Knit.

From this point, the cowl is worked back-and-forth in rows.
Row 34 [WS]: Purl.
Row 35 [RS]: K7, C12R, *k6, C12R; rep from * to last st, k1.
Rows 36-42: Work even in stockinette.
Row 43 [RS]: K1, C12L, *k6, C12L; rep from * to last 7 sts, k7.
Row 44: Purl.
Row 45 (inc row): K10, *m1, k18; rep from * to last 10 sts, m1, k10. 135 sts.
Row 46: Purl.
Row 47: K10, *BDK, k18; rep from * to last 11 sts, BDK, k10.
Rows 48-50: Work even.
Row 51: K7, *BDK, k5, BDK, k12; rep from * to last 8 sts, BDK, k7.
Rows 52-53: Purl.

At the end of Row 53, cut the yarn in preparation for the last two rows and the beaded bind off. String 67 beads on the doubled yarn and rejoin to body of piece at the same place where it was cut off. Resume knitting beg with a WS row.

Rows 54-55: Purl.
Work beaded bind off as foll: P1, *BUB, p1, bind off 1, p1, bind off 1; rep from * until all beads are placed, p1 and bind off the last stitch. If planning to work the crochet edging for the split yoke, do not cut yarn.

FINISHING
Crochet edging (optional)
Using the large crochet hook and beg with the last loop remaining from the bind off, work [1 sc, 1 ch st] up to the center of the split and back down again. Tie off.

Weave in all loose ends. Steam block lightly, concentrating on smoothing out the lower border of the yoke, and the beaded cast off.

The beaded cast on edge at the top of the neck is intended to curl, hiding and revealing the beads in a varying pattern.

VARIATIONS ON A THEME

Here are some ideas for modifications to Ms. Prynne and for additional projects using the same stitches

1. Omit beads for a plainer look.
2. Knit piece entirely in the round, remembering to change purl rows to knit rows, and increasing a few additional sts so that the yoke will lie flat over the shoulder.
3. Add more beads, applying randomly throughout the woven cable sections, or heavily beading the triangle A's in the border.

Dimmesdale Scarf

1. Cast on 47 sts and using the woven cable stitch, three repetitions across, knit until piece is desired length and bind off. The edges will curl.
2. For a more structured scarf, cast on 47 sts, and knit three rows of garter st. On the next row, increase by 8 sts, and knit the rows with 2 sts garter, 2 sts rev st st, woven cable pattern over 47 sts, 2 sts rev st st, and 2 sts garter. Work to desired length. After decreasing 8 sts evenly across the next row, end with three rows of garter stitch and bind off.
3. For a neckwarmer, knit scarf of desired width and before binding off, fold over the end (as many inches as the scarf is wide) to the wrong side and knit it in place by picking up and binding off. End of scarf tucks through loop when worn.

Little Pearl's Madcap

Cast on as for Ms. Prynne (with or without beads) and join to knit in the round. Using the woven cable pattern, knit to desired crown height, decreasing cable from 10 sts, to 8, to 6 to create shaping, ending with plain decrease rows. To finish, run thread through last row of stitches and gather up, embellishing the top with a button, a bobble, or a tassel, beaded or not.

The Leech's Pouch

Using any of the toe-up sock cast ons, cast on and knit a few rows increasing quickly to 60 or 70 sts. Switch to cable 10-stitch pattern and knit to desired size. Bind off. Knit 18 inches [46cm] or so of I-cord for drawstring and thread through cables. Use for collecting mysterious herbs.

BEADING HELP

String beads (premeditated placement)

Thread the working end of your yarn through eye of beading needle (or dental floss holder, or a loop of dental floss). Insert point of beading needle through bead, picking up a few at a time. Push the beads down onto the yarn. Continue until desired number of beads are strung.

Place beads with hook (on the fly)

Slip hook end of tiny steel crochet hook through the bead. Transfer the stitch to be beaded from the left hand needle to the hook and push the bead down onto the stitch. Return the now-beaded stitch to the left hand needle and purl the stitch. Lucy Neatby has a lovely tutorial on this.

Placing beads on the fly tutorial—http://www.youtube.com/watch?v=t77pmmqCmr4

ON THE **WWMDFK?** WEBSITE:

We have so much to be thankful for in our modern world – for one thing, we've (mostly) done away with pillories! But we haven't done away with good wholesome food like Indian Pudding, both regular and gluten free.

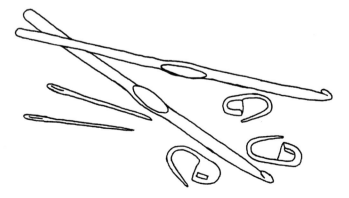

Wilhelmina Shawlette

DRACULA
Bram Stoker

Ah, *Dracula*. Who can resist this pioneering epic tale of the original blood–sucking bad boy? While the current trend is to "humanize" vampires, allowing them to feast on synthetic (*True Blood*'s Bill Compton) or animal blood (*Twilight*'s Cullen family) to make their relationships with humans more palatable, Dracula has no such delicacy. While the 1992 movie adaptation, starring the hugly (ugly yet strangely hot) Gary Oldman as the Count, takes some artistic license and attempts to humanize Dracula by telling of the death of his wife and his subsequent pursuit of Mina as his wife's doppelganger, the book makes little attempt to explain Dracula and thus keeps him delightfully and purely evil and terrifying. Don't get me wrong—I adore the movie and find both the *True Blood* and *Twilight* series to be great fun, but sometimes it's nice to just let evil be evil. Black and white. Sucking blood = bad, no sparkles or vampiric efforts of self control necessary.

The reluctant heroine of our story, Miss Wilhelmina (Mina) Murray, is obviously the inspiration for her namesake shawl design. Mina is an assistant schoolmistress whose life is turned upside down as the people closest to her (her BFF Lucy and her fiancé Jonathan) fall prey to the evil Count. While Mina's fiancé is held captive in Dracula's castle, the Count torments Lucy, feasting on her blood and eventually turning her into a vampire. Mina follows Lucy on one of her sleepwalking jaunts, discovering Lucy on a stone bench near the local graveyard, reclining in the moonlight with a dark figure bending over her. When Mina reaches Lucy, the figure is gone and Lucy appears to be asleep. Mina throws her shawl around Lucy and takes her home, assuming that the two small dots on her throat are the result of pricks from the shawl pin. After all, what else could they be?

I picture Mina as a knitter, and her unassuming practicality would support wool as her fiber of choice (of course, this is a flight of fancy as there's absolutely no reference in the book to Mina, or anyone else, knitting anything—they had bigger things on their minds, I suppose). While the shawl that Mina used to cover Lucy's neck after her midnight encounter with Dracula was described as "a big, heavy shawl" and not the lacy shawlette I've designed here, our Wilhelmina Shawlette could indeed be the perfect item to conceal delicate white necks from lustful vampire eyes or, once the deed is done (since lacy wool certainly can't compete with vampire mind control), covering up those pesky fang marks. And of course, if you wish to knit the shawl in a heavier yarn you will, indeed, wind up with a big, heavy, shawl.

After the "death" (and subsequent beheading and staking) of her dear friend, Mina assists her new husband, Jonathan, Lucy's devastated trio of suitors, and Professor Van Helsing in researching and tracking down Dracula. Inevitably, she is chewed on by the count and forced to drink his blood. As she turns from human to vampire, she establishes a psychic connection with her ghoulish boyfriend and uses it to help the hunters track him back to his Transylvanian castle, chop off his head and ultimately free Mina from her curse. And, of course, everyone lives happily ever after. Far away.

While Bram Stoker was not the first to write of vampires, his epic novel of Count Dracula is arguably the jumping–off point of most contemporary vampire and horror fiction. Whether you love or hate the idea of moral vampires, unabashed evil, good girls and bad boys, it's always fun to go back to where it all got started. And while you're there reading, a good shawl will help keep away the inevitable chills that will run up and down your spine.

—Chrissy

ON THE WWMDFK? WEBSITE:

Feeling thirsty? Try Wilhelmina's Blood Red Cordial to keep up your strength!

WILHELMINA SHAWLETTE
Designed by Chrissy Gardiner

What would Mina, the heroine of Bram Stoker's epic novel, Dracula, wear to protect her neck from the bloodthirsty count? As a practical girl, she undoubtedly would appreciate this simple, delicate wool shawlette, featuring Serendipitous Ewe's Autumn Glow, a vampire–inspired colorway, one in a series dyed exclusively for SandraSingh.com.

FINISHED MEASUREMENTS
44in wide x 22in tall [112cm x 56cm]

MATERIALS
- Serendipitous Ewe Fate Fingering [100% superwash wool; 400yd/36mm per 115g skein; 12 WPI], 1 skein Autumn Glow
- US 4 [3.5mm] circular needle, 24in [60cm] or longer
- Stitch markers

Egalité

GAUGE
28 sts and 32 rows = 4in [10cm] in stockinette. Gauge is not critical for this project.

PATTERN BEGINS
Pattern Set-up
Cast on 5 sts.
Row 1 [RS]: K2, yo, k1, yo, k2. 7 sts.
Row 2: Knit.
Row 3: K2, yo, [k1, yo] three times, k2. 11 sts.
Row 4: K2, purl to last 2 sts, k2.
Row 5: K2, pm, yo, k3, yo, pm, k1, pm, yo, k3, yo, pm, k2. 15 sts.
Row 6: K2, purl to last 2 sts, k2.
Row 7: K2, sl m, yo, k5, yo, sl m, k1, sl m, yo, k5, yo, sl m, k2. 19 sts.
Row 8: Rep Row 6.
Row 9: K2, sl m, yo, k7, yo, sl m, k1, sl m, yo, k7, yo, sl m, k2. 23 sts.
Row 10: Rep Row 6.
Row 11: K2, sl m, [yo, k1] twice, ssk, k1, k2tog, [k1, yo] twice, sl m, k1, sl m, [yo, k1] twice, ssk, k1, k2tog, [k1, yo] twice, sl m, k2. 27 sts.
Row 12: Rep Row 6.

Beg working Lace Pattern from Chart A, repeating Rows 1-20 a total of 4 times. 187 sts. Then, work Rows 1-18 of Lace Pattern once more. 223 sts.

Note: The sts will be distributed across the rows between markers as foll — two border sts worked in garter st (knitted every row), marker #1, Lace Patt over a varying number of sts to marker #2, one center st worked in St st, marker #3, Lace Patt over a varying number of sts to marker #4, two border sts worked in garter st. 4 sts will be added on every RS row.

The outlined box indicates the pattern repeat. The shaded stitch (#34, in chart A) is the center stitch of the shawl.

Edging
Work Edging Rows 1-22 from Chart B. Edge and center sts are not charted; continue working them as established, working the charted pattern between the markers. Outlined box indicates pattern repeat. 245 sts.

FINISHING
Bind off all sts as foll: K1, *yo, k1; pass 2nd and 3rd sts on right needle over 1st st on right needle (one st rem on right needle); rep from * until all sts are bound off.

Weave in all ends and block by soaking briefly in cool water and mild detergent or wool wash. Gently squeeze water from shawl and roll in towels, or spin in top-loading washing machine to remove excess moisture. Spread damp shawl out on clean surface such as a bed or flat towels and pin into shape. For best results, use blocking wires to make top edge nice and straight and lower edges nicely scalloped. Let dry completely.

Chart A (lace pattern)

CHART B (EDGING CHART)

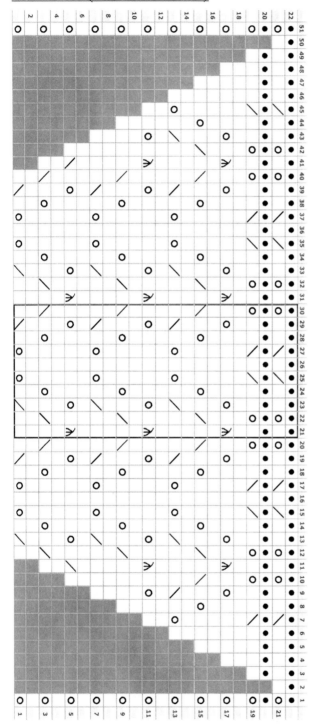

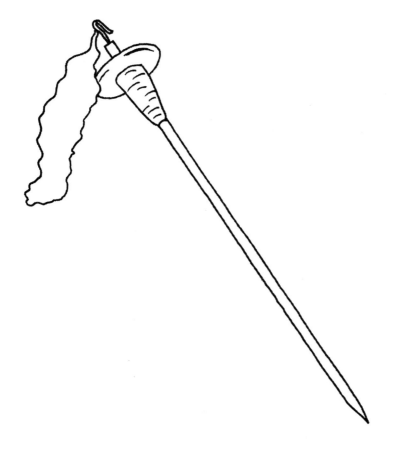

A TALE OF TWO CITIES
Charles Dickens

Yes, Madame Defarge is technically a villain. But she's also really cool. Smart, driven, (vengeful, sure, but we'll leave that aside for now), passionate, and she has a cause worth dying for.

That, and, you know, she's an awesome knitter.

When I was a high school freshman, I had a lousy English teacher who—though he couldn't inspire the sun to rise even with the help of the earth's rotation—thought he could inspire a room full of fourteen–year–olds to love Dickens' remarkable novel.

He was wrong.

I'm not sure if any of us actually read the book or if this was one of those shameful "I'll just use this small black and yellow striped booklet to help me a little" moments for most of us. I'm willing to bet it was the latter. Regardless, I went for over 25 years without cracking that tome. I was even proud of it (I did, after all, get an A on the test). But then Julie at the *Forgotten Classics* podcast wrote to me and said, "Really. You must listen to this book."

Well, Julie is not to be denied lest one risk looking foolish, so I trooped over to Librivox.org to find and listen to the audio of the book. Aside from being blown away by the sweeping story, I seem to recall sitting in the car, in the garage, with the engine off, listening to the last fifteen minutes of the book with tears blopping all over the steering wheel.

Yep. That good.

And we could go on for days about Sidney Carton and his studliness or Lucy and her inanity, or how great it is to wear a WWMDfK? t–shirt in public, but we're really here to talk about Madame Defarge, no?

There are many parts of the book I love that include the Madame and her DA DA DUMmmmmm appearances, yet I think my favorite vignette is a simple one—simple, but one about knitting, nonetheless.

Madame Defarge with her work in her hand was accustomed to pass from place to place and from group to group: a Missionary—there were many like her—such as the world will do well never to breed again. All the women knitted. They knitted worthless things; but, the mechanical work was a mechanical substitute for eating and drinking; the hands moved for the jaws and the digestive apparatus: if the bony fingers had been still, the stomachs would have been more famine–pinched.

But, as the fingers went, the eyes went, and the thoughts. And as Madame Defarge moved on from group to group, all three went quicker and fiercer among every little knot of women that she had spoken with, and left behind.

Her husband smoked at his door, looking after her with admiration. "A great woman," said he, "a strong woman, a grand woman, a frightfully grand woman!"

We'll get to the hunger thing in a sec, but first a word about the Mister. Her husband reminds me a bit of Lord Macbeth and his Lady. He probably started the whole I–wanna–be–Laird thing, but it was up to Lady M to finish it. In both *Macbeth* and *Tale*, rank admiration flows from the gentlemen directly towards their wives. Both guys also seem to have moments where they wonder if she's not perhaps a little too committed:

"Can it be true," said Defarge, in a low voice, looking down at his wife as he stood smoking with his hand on the back of her chair: "what he has said of Ma'amselle Manette?"

"As he [the spy] has said it," returned madame, lifting her eyebrows a little, "it is probably false. But it may be true."

"If it is—" Defarge began, and stopped.

"If it is?" repeated his wife.

"—And if it does come, while we live to see it triumph—I hope, for her sake, Destiny will keep her husband out of France."

"Her husband's destiny," said Madame Defarge, with her usual composure, "will take him where he is to go, and will lead him to the end that is to end him. That is all I know."

"But it is very strange—now, at least, is it not very strange"—said Defarge, rather pleading with his wife to induce her to admit it, "that, after all our sympathy for Monsieur her father, and herself, her husband's name should be proscribed under your hand at this moment, by the side of that infernal dog's who has just left us?"

"Stranger things than that will happen when it does come," answered madame. "I have them both here, of a certainty; and they are both here for their merits; that is enough."

She rolled up her knitting when she had said those words...

And with that, the Madame had condemned a good and innocent man to death, dragging her poor husband along with her.

I know. It doesn't seem like we should praise someone who could condemn another human that easily, but we also have to place her in time. She was, of course, working to end the corrupt and brutal oppressive class struggle that was the French Revolution. The book is filled with images of how poor and how hungry the people are. The first quotation in this essay shows that well enough. And I know that I'm guilty of having joked flippantly, …if only I could lose weight by knitting. But it's not really very funny, is it? It clearly wasn't to the Madame—more fuel for her passion, though.

John Adams is said to have written: There are only two creatures of value on the face of the earth: those with commitment, and those who require the commitment of others. Well, Madame Defarge was a portrait of commitment. Martin Luther King said, prophetically, "A man who won't die for something isn't fit to live." Some days I wonder if, aside from my family, there is anything I believe in enough that I would be willing to lay down my life for it? Any abstract belief that I carry in my heart with such conviction that I would sacrifice myself to see those ends met?

I can't think of anything.

I wonder how life would change if the things I profess to believe in, I believed in to the extent that I'd risk everything for that cause. What would it be like to live the way Madame Defarge lives? Would the world be a better place? Would we all be exhausted? Is that kind of fervor reserved for the young, for the not–yet–raising–children? Is it only the very few of us who can sustain that level of passion—of valor—even when there are mouths to feed and dishes to wash?

I don't know. And I don't know that I'd want to live in that world. But I do know this: Whatever it was, I have a lot of respect for (and some healthy fear of) whatever Madame Defarge Knits.

—Heather

MADAME DEFARGE'S STOLE
Designed by Heather Ordover with Wendy McDonnell

Dickens doesn't give us a lot of help when figuring out what exactly Madame Defarge was up to. We know a few things: what she was knitting could be mistaken for a shroud, it was of her own creation, it was abstract enough to be taken as a "design" from a short distance. When designing a piece in her name I wrestled with what she might actually have knitted given the time and available techniques—which would mean you would have had to memorize something resembling the Braille alphabet (which the French Revolution, however, predated by 32 years). That hardly seemed pleasant, though bobbles certainly make it possible.

I also wanted to make sure that the stole could we worn by anyone for any occasion, knitting in wedding dates, birthdates, christening dates, or names of those we love. Thus, once I sat down to actually begin the design process, I knew I wanted delicate wine glasses and the artfully trellised windows of her shop, tear–drop leaves both as a symbol of renewal and for the lives lost in the revolution, and ruffles both feminine (because she had once been beautiful) and severe all represented. I wanted the stole to be attractive enough to be worn easily by anyone, but at the same time I needed to find a way to hide a message within all of the loveliness. Just as the Madame had her Ernst as a helpmeet, I also found aid from two men.

Franklin Habit of *The Panopticon* turned me on to Bridget Rorem's Lace Alphabets from Schoolhouse Press Pattern #9. Rorem's garter stitch letters are no less than brilliant, but for this project they didn't work as written according to the vast number of swatches I made. For a smooth surface (because, we should be honest, the Madame was a smooth operator in her line of business) the stole needed to be knit stockinette. The other challenge was that the original letters were not of uniform width and for the purposes of our stole (and the sanity of our knitters) we needed uniformity. While I have used Rorem's genius as a starting point, what you find here is an alphabet altered for our own revolution. Use your letters with care and discretion as the Madame did. If you wish to maximize your options, I heartily recommend you scoot over to Schoolhouse Press' website and procure a copy of SPP #9. You will not be disappointed.

I did say that there were two men who helped inspire me — I didn't forget. The words coded into the back of the stole are invisible unless the stole is pulled taut and are courtesy of my husband, who also loves the Madame.

The two samples of this stole were knit in wine-red laceweight yarn from Schoppel Wolle with long oak-leaf edges and the other in white Goddess Lace merino 2-ply with daggered edges. The white example shows how lovely the stole might be if used for a birthday or Christening celebration. Instructions after the pattern have been provided by Wendy McDonnell for dyeing the stole a tasteful blood and wine red.

— Heather

FINISHED MEASUREMENTS
Center and side panels knitted per instructions, with upper and lower ruffles but without side edgings: 20in tall x 71in wide [51cm x 180cm]; total width will depend on edging

MATERIALS
 [MC] Schoppel-Wolle Zauberball [75% wool, 25% nylon; 876yd/800m per 100g skein; 23 WPI], 2 balls #1872 Plum Sauce

Fraternité

Stole as knitted used about 1000yds/910m.

US 5 [3.75mm] circular needle, 40in [100cm] long
 Stitch markers

Consider using hair elastics for the many markers you will use on the center panel. Scünci makes a silicone model which slips along the needles nicely.)

GAUGE
Approx. 18 sts and 27 rows = 4in [10cm] in stockinette, blocked hard vertically

PATTERN NOTES
The construction of this stole is slightly different from others you may have knit, but it avoids grafting at the end. You will begin by using two balls (or both inner and outer strands from one ball) to knit both side panels. Your needle will look like this when the side panels are done. If you loathe picking up stitches, you may want to use a provisional cast-on for the center and side panels. See the directions that begin on page 166.

PATTERN BEGINS
Side Panels (2)

Cast on 82 sts over two needles held together (for looseness) with one ball of yarn, then cast on another 82 sts with second ball of yarn (or other end from same ball). Purl 1 row. Begin working Chart A, orienting your work as per fig. 1. Be careful to keep yarns separate. Work the 28 rows of Chart A twice.

Note that only RS rows are shown on the chart. Purl all WS rows. Outlined box shows the pattern repeat.

CHART A

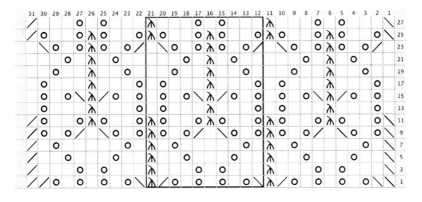

At end of Chart A, work panels as foll:
Row 1 [WS]: Purl.
Row 2 [RS]: Knit.

Row 3: Purl.
Row 4: K2tog twice, *yo, k2tog; rep from * to
end. 80 sts each panel.
Row 5: Purl across first (left) panel only. Cut
the yarn leaving an 8in [20cm] tail. Purl
across second (right) panel, do not cut yarn.
Row 6 (first row Chart B): Knit to end of
right panel, cast on 180 sts placing markers as
indicated by section breaks of Chart B, turn.

> **On the WWMDfK? website:**
>
> *Seeing Red? Have some
> Strawberries in Red with
> Black Pepper Sauce to
> compare.*

PLEASE NOTE: Chart B is very, very large
and can be downloaded from the WWMDfK? website to save both pages and your sanity.

Center Panel

As you join the center panel to the side panels it is important to keep your seaming stitches
(the p2togs and k3togs at the ends of the rows) very loose. If you don't, then blocking will
strain the knitting. There are variations on the height of the panel — made by adjusting
the seamed stitches — at the end of this section.

To work joins at each end of every WS row (see special note for Row 2, below), purl the
first (or last) stitch of the center panel together with one stitch from the side panel.
To work joins at each end of every RS row, work the first (or last) two stitches of the center
panel together with one stitch from the side panel, using k3tog or s2kp, as chart indicates.

Both RS and WS rows are shown on
Chart B. Row 1 is the cast-on row you
just completed at the end of the last
section.

To work the first join on Row 2 [WS]: Sl1
from right-hand needle to left (you are
slipping a stitch from the original left
panel). Place marker on right needle.
P2tog using both the working yarn and
the 8in [20cm] tail held together. Work
the rest of the row as charted.

You may wish to block the stole lightly
after finishing Chart B. This will open up
the knitting and make it easier to pick up
the many stitches needed for the next
stage.

> *Add height option: You may work
> Rows 3-18 and 68-81 a second
> time to create a taller stole. Doing
> so will add about 6in [15cm] of
> height. You will not need to change
> the side panels; just adjust the
> number of joining stitches so that
> on every third row (throughout
> the center panel) you skip the join
> by working ssk or k2tog instead of
> s2kp or k3tog at the beginning
> and end (RS rows), and purl the
> first and last stitches plain instead
> of working p2tog at the beginning
> and end (WS rows)*

Edgings Set-up

After completing Chart B, you should have 180 live stitches along the top edge of the stole. With RS facing, pick up and knit 53 sts from the top of the left side panel, pick up 2 sts from the top left corner, pm, pick up another 3 sts from the same corner st, pick up 82 sts down the side of the stole, pick up 3 sts from the bottom left corner, pm, pick up 2 sts from the same corner st, pick up 286 sts along the bottom edge, pick up 2 sts from the bottom right corner, pm, pick up 3 sts from the same corner st, pick up 82 sts up the right side of the stole, pick up 3 sts from the top right corner, pm of different color for beg of rnd. Pick up and knit 2 sts from the same corner st, pick up 53 sts across top of right side panel. Knit around to the beg-of-rnd marker. 756 sts; 88 on each short side and 290 on each long side.

> *How do you pick up 4 or 5 sts from just one stitch? It is easiest to do this as though doing Cat Bordhi's Mobius cast-on; minute marker 1:20 begins the demonstration of the swinging motion you can use to make multiple stitches in a single corner stitch.*

Rnd 1: *Yo, k2tog; rep from * to end.
Rnd 2: Knit.
Rnd 3: *K2tog, yo; rep from * to end.
Rnd 5: Knit.

Top Ruffle

Begin by knitting from the beg-of-rnd marker across to the top left corner marker. Turn to begin working on a WS row. The top ruffle is worked only on the 290 sts between the two markers of the top corners.

CHART C (UPPER RUFFLE)

	27	26	25	24	23	22	21	20	19	18	17	16	15	14	13	12	11	10	9	8	7	6	5	4	3	2	1	
		•	M							•	•	M						•	•					M				10
9				•						•	•							•	•									
		•	M							•	•	M						•	•					M				8
7					•					•	•							•	•									
				•	M					•	•	M						•	•				M					6
5						•					•	•						•	•									
					•	M					•	•	M					•	•			M						4
3							•				•	•						•	•									
						•	M				•	•	M					•	•	M								2
1								•				•	•					•	•									

Outlined box shows the pattern repeat. Row 1 is a WS row.

Chart E (lower ruffle)

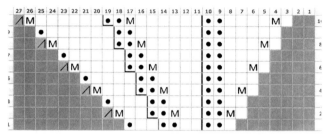

After completing Row 10 of Chart C, bind off in pattern. Do not fasten off, but leave the last stitch live at the upper right corner. WS facing, rotate the work and pick up and purl 9 sts down the side of the ruffle in preparation for the right side edging.

This is a fairly short ruffle. You can lengthen it if desired by continuing the pattern as established, adding another m1 on each RS row. A taller ruffle at the top of the stole will be somewhat floppy; on the bottom edge it would drape nicely.

Right Side Edging (Oak Leaves)
You will work Chart D back-and-forth, beginning with the 10 sts currently attached to the top ruffle. As you knit, you will join the edging to the 88 live sts along the right side of the stole by working together 1 st from the stole with 1 st from the edging at the beg of every RS row. The chart shows this as sl1, k1, psso; since you have the live stole sts already on your right needle, all you need do is k1 from the edging, pass 1 stole st over.

Work the 16 rows of Chart D 11 times, ending with WS facing. Row 1 is a RS row.

Lower Ruffle
The Lower Ruffle is knit much the same as the Upper Ruffle, over the 290 sts between the markers on the bottom edge of the stole, with the difference that you must join the right edge of the ruffle to the end of the oak leaf edging as you go by knitting 1 ruffle stitch together with 2 stitches from the end of the oak leaf edging at the end of every RS row.

Chart D (oak leaves, right)

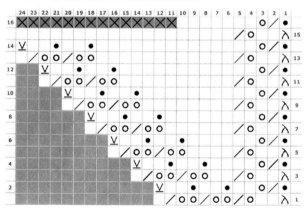

Row 1 is a WS row. After completing Row 10 of Chart E, bind off in pattern. Break yarn.

Chart F (oak leaves, left)

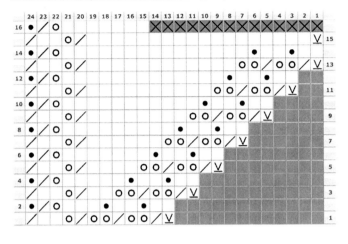

Left Side Edging (Oak Leaves)
The left side edging is made like the right side, working from the top edge of the stole down. The joins are at the end of each RS row. Begin by joining yarn to left corner of upper ruffle where it meets the body of the stole, WS facing; pick up and purl 10 sts up ruffle edge.

Row 1 of Chart F is a RS row. Work the 16 rows of Chart F 11 times. Graft the rem sts loosely to the side of the lower ruffle.

FINISHING
Block carefully, pinning ruffles in place along top and lower edges. Weave in any ends. Enjoy!

DAGGER EDGING VARIATION
by Wendy McDonnell, aka Yarn Fairy

"Tell the Wind and the Fire where to stop; not me!"
—Madame DeFarge. (Vol. 3, chap. 12, para. 36)
Can you not see the dagger on her lap, there just peeking out from under her knitting? This edging is worked over 90 stitches. To use the dagger chart instead of the oak leaves, begin with one set of side sts, join yarn with WS facing. Purl 1 row, inc across evenly to make 90 sts.

Follow Chart G (next page). You will be working on 15 sts at a time, knitting out from the body of the stole. The rest of the stitches stay on the needle until they are needed. You may find it easier to work the daggers on two double pointed or straight needles, leaving the stitches not in use on the circular needle.

Fasten off at the end of the chart and rejoin yarn to the next set of 15 sts. Repeat until you have six daggers. Row 1 is a RS row. The top and bottom ruffles are left loose.

DYEING OPTIONS
Instructions by Wendy McDonnell

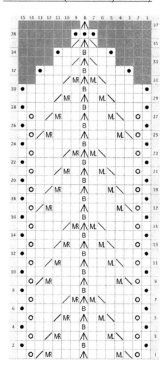

Red for the blood that lavishly flowed through the streets of France, purple for the aristocrats who provided that blood, lastly, black for the death that followed in the wake of... La Guillotine. And all the while, Madame Defarge and Les Tricoteuses right there out in front, knitting the names of the doomed.

PREP WORK FOR DYEING

If you have never dyed before I highly recommend you watch a tutorial[5] about dyeing with an acid based dye. Paying special attention to handling the dye in the process with use of gloves, masks, drop cloths, food prep areas, then the clean up with a 50/50 solution of bleach/water for your kitchen.

Don't be intimidated, though. You can absolutely do this. It's not as daunting as it sounds. For small amounts of dye, try KnitPicks.com or DharmaTrading.com.

These instructions will walk you through a three–tone dying adventure. For this stole we used red, blue, and black dye. With the stole open and the right side facing, fold the stole in half by bringing daggers together, then in half again to create a packet of fabric narrow enough to fit into your stock pot without a struggle. Using a dowel or chopstick and a piece of sturdy woolen yarn, whip stitch through the top ruffle and all layers to loosely attach the stole to your dowel.

- Make sure it's loose enough for the dye to move freely between the layers, yet tight enough so that it will not fall off of the stick. If you keep your sewing straight you should get a hard line for the red to blue. Or you will have the "blood" curving through the street as you see in mine.
- Whip stitch with large basting stitch through daggers 2 at a time, (oak leaf–4, 4, 3) both left and right sides and through the stole folds (see photo). Sew these layers together to match the increments of the dye stages (in this case the stages were red, blue, black) so the daggers stay with their line or dye rather than dropping into a lower dye stage.
- Tie another string on to the right of the stick then loop over to the left and tie off again on the stick, this is your hanger. A wire hanger would work too if it will fit in your pot.
- This string (and stick) has to set into the pot at different heights while you are dip

dyeing your stole so make sure you have a place to tie the handle off above the pot on your stove. For example, on your cabinet handle, hinge or vent hood, anything sturdy up above which you can loop a string over.

Soak your stole in a container overnight in a mixture of 3/4 room temperature water and 1/4 vinegar—enough to cover the stole without forcing it. Red dye is known for running which is why we use so much vinegar. You don't really need a large container for this, just large enough for the stole to move freely. We use a small plastic tote box.

DIP DYEING YOUR STOLE

Wearing good rubber gloves, mix well, 1 teaspoon of an acid based red dye, such as Jacquard, with 1 cup of hot water. We use old yoghurt containers for this part of the process. Our red is Jacquard Fire Red #618.

Remove the stole from its soak and put the soak water into a large pot like a retired water bath canner (never again to be used for food) or some other old pot. Add another cup of vinegar to the pot and the red dye mix you made.

Place the entire stole into the red dye. Gently open the layers so that all of the yarn is allowed to come into contact with the color. Turn on the heat, bring up to a boil and immediately turn down to simmer on low for 20–30 minutes or until you are satisfied with the top edge color. Keep in mind that red is notorious for bleeding and that wet yarn "reads" darker so it might end up a shade or two lighter then the color it is in the pot.

Pull the stole out about one third of the way and tie off. This is where ingenuity and string over a cabinet door can be used to help to hold the stole in place.

While the pot is simmering, mix well, 1/2 teaspoon of deep blue dye with 1 cup of hot water.

Add the blue dye to the red bath; ours is Sapphire Blue #622. Leave in for about 20–30 minutes, still at a low simmer. Do not pour the dye onto the stole but into the water, stir well without agitating the stole. Make sure that all the yarn comes in contact with the dye.

Mix well, ½ teaspoon of black with 1 cup of hot water.

Pull the stole another third of the way out and tie off.

Add the black dye (ours is Jet Black #639), leave in for about 20–30 minutes. Make sure that all the yarn comes in contact with the dye.

THE PERFECT ENDING

Remove the stole from the pot, cut all strings, and allow it to cool completely with little movement. When totally cooled off, place stole into a room temperature water bath, rinse till all excess dye is gone. If you experience dye run off, drain water completely out of stole, place into bowl, pour straight vinegar over it until the stole is saturated completely. Heat in microwave 1 minute, turn. Continue this process until hot (this will depend on your microwave's strength—use your judgement and decrease cook time as necessary), allow to cool. Wash with a hair shampoo and conditioner. I find that the Suave Kiwi will leave "pixy dust" behind if you don't rinse really well, a very nice touch at the end. Block and enjoy!

CONSTRUCTION NOTES

For a quick overview of chart placement, please refer to the below:

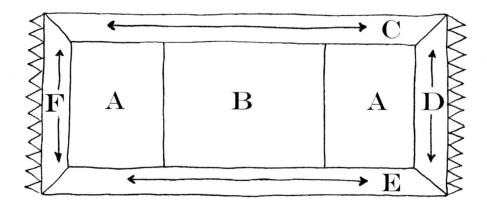

The construction of this shawl is slightly different from others you may have knit, but it avoids grafting at the end. You will begin using two balls (or both inner and outer strands from one ball) to knit both side panels. Your needle will look like this when the side panels are done.

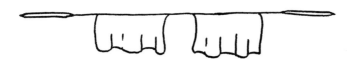

You will then drop the yarn of the panel to your left (RS) and cast on in between the panels. Knit back and forth, joining (seaming) the new center panels to the side panels by loosely p2tog at ach edge of every wrong side row and loosely k3tog at each edge of every right side row. As you knit the central panel, your knitting will begin to look like this as you gradually join the center panels to the side panels.

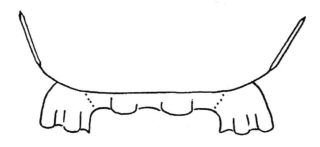

Lysistrata

LYSISTRATA
Aristophanes

Lysistrata, the title character in the fourth–century (BCE) play by Aristophanes, is my kind of woman. A rabble–rouser and apple cart upsetter of the first order, she is instrumental in ending a senseless war between Sparta and Athens that has raged for thirty years. Her weapon of choice: sex—specifically, the withholding thereof. All she has to do is convince the rest of the women of Greece that this is what they want, too.

Initially reluctant to take part in the bold plan, the women of Greece eventually come around once Lysistrata explains that that they are living under a form of tyranny; forced to live without their husbands for extended periods of time, they are denied a voice in the proceedings surrounding the war, and even forbidden from hearing discussion of the wars that rob them of their loved ones. With Lysistrata's impassioned speech the women unite and, with solemn vows around a shared wine bowl, agree to remain celibate until the war ends. Under Lysistrata's canny guidance, the women also seize the Acropolis, the repository of the state treasury, without which the men cannot continue to fund their war.

The ensuing battle of wills between the sexes is rude, lewd and bawdy, with Greek choruses and double entendres aplenty, as about half of the women are ready to desert the cause, finding ever more preposterous ways to slink off and break their vow of celibacy. Happily, there are enough strong women left to keep the weak willed among their sisters in line and, at the same time, suggestively drive their own husbands to distraction. The poor men, lacking the money to continue their war, and now highly motivated to end it, agree to settle their grievances.

At the end of the play, as Lysistrata brokers the peace treaty between Sparta and Athens, she warns both sides that she is well–schooled in politics, despite having been denied the right to discuss it publicly all these years. She lectures both the Athenians and Spartans, likening them to barbarians for killing one another, and peace is declared at last.

Though written 2300 years before the rise of modern feminism Aristophanes has, albeit inadvertently, crafted in Lysistrata both a story of successful pacifism, and a feminist icon for the ages. It is Lysistrata who sees what the men in the story do not, the futility of endless conflict, and Lysistrata who devises a peaceful yet cunning plan to end it. It is Lysistrata who leads the women of Greece, and Lysistrata who must protect these same women from their own worst instincts in order to accomplish her mission. Lysistrata who, at the end of the play, claims a power equal to that of men, based not on sex or coercion, but on the merits of her own intelligence.

— Brenda

LYSISTRATA'S CHITON
Designed by Brenda Dayne

Little more than a rectangle of cloth drawn up at the shoulders and pinned, the chiton was for centuries the garment favored by the ancient Greeks. No less beautiful for its simplicity, Lysistrata's Chiton is, likewise, based on the functional rectangle, with the addition of raglan sleeves, both shapely and flattering. Knit sideways to maximize drape of the knitted fabric the cardigan features a wide organic cable flanking both fronts and hugging the neck, while softly draping folds of fabric fall, chiton–like, from the shoulders.

SIZE
S [M, L]

Liberté

FINISHED MEASUREMENTS
Full width 44 [48, 52]in [112 (122, 132)cm]
Back width at bust 22 [24, 26]in [56 (61, 66)cm]
Length 20 [22, 24]in [51 (56, 61)cm]

MATERIALS
➤ Briar Rose Fibers Wistful [50% alpaca, 50% merino wool, 20% silk; 500yd/457m per 227g skein; 13 WPI], 3 [4, 4] skeins
➤ US 8 [5mm] needles
➤ Stitch markers
➤ Stitch holders or waste yarn
➤ Cable needle

GAUGE
20 sts and 24 rows = 4in [10cm] in stockinette

STITCH GUIDE
M1yo: Worked over 2 rows. On first row, yo at point of increase. On second row, yo again at point of increase, then knit or purl the previous row's yo through the back loop to twist the stitch. 2 sts inc'd over 2 rows.

Cable Pattern (panel of 24 sts)
Row 1 [RS]: K12, sl6 to cable needle and hold in front of work, k6, k6 from cable needle.
Rows 2-6: Purl all sts on WS rows and knit all sts on RS rows.
Row 7: Rep Row 1.
Rows 8-12: Purl all on WS rows and knit all on RS rows.
Row 13: Sl6 to cable needle and hold in back of work, k6, k6 from cable needle.
Rows 15-18: Purl all on WS rows and knit all on RS rows.
Row 19: Rep Row 13.
Rows 21-24: Purl all on WS rows and knit all on RS rows.
Rep Rows 1-24.

PATTERN NOTES
Body is knit side-to-side in one piece. Sleeves are knit separately and seamed. See schematic on page 171 for section locations.

PATTERN BEGINS
Section 1
Cast on 100 [110, 120] sts.
Rows 1-6: Knit.
Row 7 [RS]: K4, pm, k24, pm, knit to last 8 sts, pm, k8.
Row 8 [WS]: K8, purl to second marker, k4.
Row 9: K4, sl m, work Row 1 of cable pattern over next 24 sts, sl m, knit to end.
Row 10: K8, purl to first marker, work Row 2 of cable pattern over next 24 sts, k4.
Continue as established by last two rows, with garter st borders at each end and cable over 24 marked sts, until piece measures 11 [12, 13]in [28 (30.5, 33)cm] from cast on, ending with a WS row.

Next row [RS]: Work 61 [63, 65] sts in patt, k2tog, k1, turn. Place rem 36 [44, 52] sts on a holder.

Section II
Next row [WS]: Sl1, p2tog, work in patt to end.
Next row [RS]: Work to last 3 sts, k2tog, k1.
Dec on every row as set until 28 sts rem.
Work even 5 rows, ending with a RS row. Place sts on a holder.

Section III
Replace the 36 [44, 52] held sts on needle. With RS facing join yarn, bind off 5 sts, work in patt to end. 31 [39, 47] sts. Work 5 rows even ending with a WS row.

Next row [RS]: Sl1, k1, m1yo, work to end.
Next row [WS]: Work in patt to last 2 sts, m1yo, p2.
Inc on every row as set to 67 [77, 87] sts.
Work 1 RS row even.

Joining row [WS]: Work across all Section III sts in patt, cast on 5 sts, sl 28 sts from holder to left needle, work across these sts in patt to complete row. 100 [110, 120] sts.

Section IV
Work even for 8 [9.5, 11]in [20.5 (24.5, 28)cm], ending with a RS row.

Section V
Next row [WS]: Work 67 [77, 87] sts in pattern, then place on stitch holder. Bind off 5 sts, work rem 28 sts in patt to complete row. Work 5 rows even, ending with a RS row.

Next row [WS]: Sl1, p1, m1yo, work to end.

Next row [RS]: Work in patt to last 3 sts, m1yo, k2.
Inc on every row as set to 64 [66, 68] sts.
Place these sts on a holder.

Section VI
Replace 67 [77, 87] sts from holder on needle. With RS facing, join yarn and work in patt to end.

Next row [WS]: Work in patt to last 3 sts, ssp, p1.
Next row [RS]: Sl1, ssk, work to end.
Dec on every row as set until 31 [39, 47] sts rem.
Work 6 rows even, ending with a RS row.

Joining row: With WS facing, work across all sts in pattern, cast on 5 sts, sl 64 [66, 68] sts from holder to left needle, work across all sts in patt to complete row. 100 [110, 120] sts.

Section VII
Work even for 10 [11, 12]in [25.5 (28, 30.5)cm] ending with a RS row.
Knit 6 rows. Bind off.

Sleeves
Cast on 46 sts. Knit 6 rows. Work in stockinette beg with a RS row for 8 rows.
Inc row [RS]: K2, m1, knit to last 2 sts, m1, k2.
Continue in stockinette, inc as set by last row on every 8th row 7 [0, 0] times, then on every 6th row 6 [14, 10] times, then every 4th row 0 [2, 9] times. 74 [80, 84] sts.
Work even until sleeve measures 17 [17.5, 18]in [43 (44.5, 45.5)cm], ending with a WS row.

Cap shaping
Bind off 6 sts at beg of next 2 rows. 62 [68, 72] sts.
Next row [RS]: K2, k2tog, knit to last 4 sts, ssk, k2.
Next row [WS]: P2, ssp, purl to last 4 sts, p2tog, p2.
Dec on every row as set until 32 [30, 30] sts rem, then on RS rows only until 12 sts rem.
Work 1 row even.
Bind off.

FINISHING
Block pieces. Sew sleeve underarm seams.
Set sleeves into armholes, matching underarm seams to X on schematic. Weave in ends.

Schematic

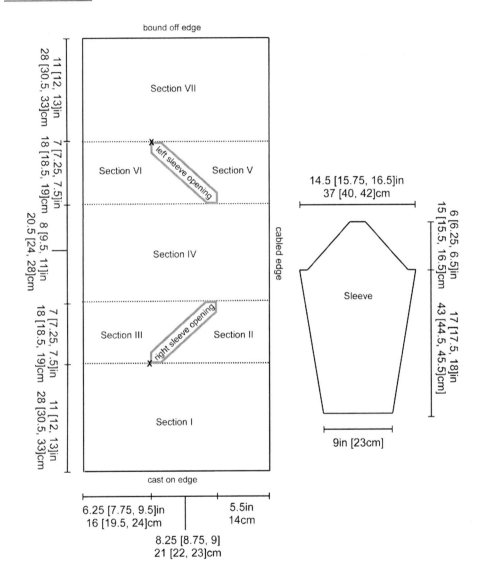

bound off edge

Section VII

Section VI   left sleeve opening   Section V

Section IV

Section III   right sleeve opening   Section II

Section I

cast on edge

cabled edge

11 [12, 13]in
28 [30.5, 33]cm

7 [7.25, 7.5]in
18 [18.5, 19]cm

8 [9.5, 11]in
20.5 [24, 28]cm

7 [7.25, 7.5]in
18 [18.5, 19]cm

11 [12, 13]in
28 [30.5, 33]cm

6.25 [7.75, 9.5]in
16 [19.5, 24]cm

5.5in
14cm

8.25 [8.75, 9]
21 [22, 23]cm

14.5 [15.75, 16.5]in
37 [40, 42]cm

Sleeve

6 [6.25, 6.5]in
15 [15.5, 16.5]cm

17 [17.5, 18]in
43 [44.5, 45.5]cm

9in [23cm]

EMMA
Jane Austen

In high school, I got busted for embroidering in class, and I read a lot of Jane Austen. In short, I wasn't exactly the rebellious type (hair color and leather jacket excepted). While *Pride and Prejudice* and other Austen novels made immediate sense to me, it took me time and maturity to absorb the messages in *Emma*. Such is the wonder of Austen — you can reread it again and again and glean something new each time.

Emma Woodhouse, handsome, clever, and rich, with a comfortable home and happy disposition, seemed to unite some of the best blessings of existence; and had lived nearly twenty-one years in the world with very little to distress or vex her.

So begins the novel, which concentrates on the matchmaking exploits of Jane Austen's most frustrating character, yet it reveals much more about its protagonist's flaws than it does of her attempts at playing Cupid. Why is she frustrating? Because Emma personifies the very worst kind of interference, that which is done presumably for one's own good.

In *Emma*, Mrs Bates (a friend of Emma's father) is always knitting, and Miss Bates, her spinster daughter, is always talking…and talking…*and talking*, causing Emma herself no small amount of annoyance. I find this hilarious, because Emma is positive she knows what's best for everyone, and that they should listen to her every pronouncement as if it were printed on golden tablets. Her opinion of herself is very high, her social skills somewhat damaged. No one likes a cocktail party bore or know-it-all. Eventually, this results in overblown jealousy directed towards the Bates' orphaned niece Jane Fairfax, an accomplished knitter with excellent manners and musical skills:

One is sick of the very name of Jane Fairfax. Every letter from her is read forty times over; her compliments to all friends go round and round again; and if she does but send her aunt the pattern of a stomacher, or knit a pair of garters for her grandmother, one hears of nothing else for a month. I wish Jane Fairfax very well; but she tires me to death.

Jane will soon be forced to work as a governess if she can't marry above her circumstances (let's not forget that in Austen's time marriage truly was the only way out of a bad socioeconomic roll of the dice for most women). Emma already has all the money and social advantages Jane does not, making her envy of Jane's talents all the more absurd, and her cruelty to the chatty Miss Bates even worse. Emma isn't someone to admire: she's a bully with very few people to keep her in check. So let's wrap ourselves up in something for Jane, who in the end does make a happy marriage, despite Emma's misguided machinations.

—Shannon

JANE FAIRFAX'S TIPPET
Designed by Shannon Okey and Andi Smith

Miss Bates, concerned for the health of young Jane, says:

Jane, Jane, my dear Jane, where are you?—Here is your tippet. Mrs. Weston begs you to put on your tippet. She says she is afraid there will be draughts in the passage, though every thing has been done.

Whether your house is drafty or not, this tippet will keep your neck toasty warm without the bulk of a scarf.

SIZE
One size

FINISHED MEASUREMENTS
Full width 17.5in, unstretched. [44.5 cm]

MATERIALS
- Bijou Basin Ranch Bijou Bliss [50% yak, 50% Cormo wool; 150yd/137m per 56g skein; 16 WPI], 1 skein
- US 10 [6mm] needles
- Stitch markers
- Stitch holders or waste yarn
- Cable needle or dpn, if desired, to work cabled stitches
- Buttons (5 used here; you may want more/less depending on your button choice)

GAUGE
28 sts and 30 rows = 4in [10cm] in stockinette

PATTERN NOTES
This neck wrap is worked from the chin down to the shoulders.

PATTERN BEGINS
Cast on 84 sts, then work a foundation row as follows:

Foundation: K4, *p6, k4; rep from * to end

Row 1: Repeat columns 1 - 10 of chart until 4 sts remain, then work columns 1 - 4
Work pattern as established, repeating rows 1 - 4 until piece measures 5 inches, then work rows 5 - 16 once

Short row shaping
Row 1: Work 20 sts in pattern as established, wrap and turn
Row 2: Work 16 sts in pattern, wrap and turn

Row 3: Work 14 sts in pattern, wrap and turn
Row 4: Work 12 sts in pattern, wrap and turn
Row 5: Work to 40th st in pattern (end of second fan shape), wrap and turn,
Rows 6-8: Repeat rows 2-4.
Row 9: Work in pattern to end
Row 10: Knit. Bind off all sts purlwise

Weave in ends, then sew each of 5 buttons 1 inch apart down front side, matching eyelet holes on opposite side as button holes. Block by lightly soaking in a wool wash such as Soak, then dry flat. Allow to dry fully before wearing.

CHART

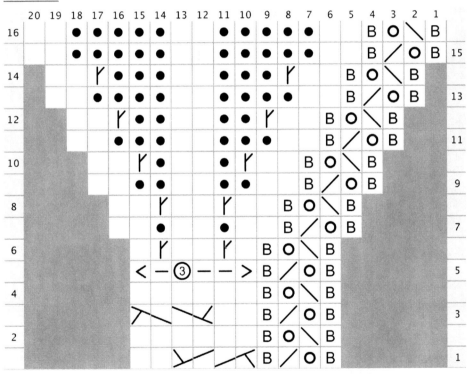

APPENDIX

Jane's Ubiquitous Shawl's appearances in Jane Eyre

While there are other shawls in the novel, I leave those for you to investigate on your own and shall address only Jane's wearing, putting on, and taking off of shawls at key turning points in her life:

CHAPTER III

Next day, by noon, I was up and dressed, and sat wrapped in a shawl by the nursery hearth

The morning after the red–room incident at Graveshead, the chilling climax of her time living there, a shawl comforts Jane, protects her, helps her heal from her terror.

CHAPTER X

I sat up in bed by way of arousing this said brain: it was a chilly night; I covered my shoulders with a shawl, and then I proceeded to think again with all my might.

Pondering her future, trying to decide whether to leave Lowood or not and what to do, considering all her options, Jane needs to brace herself to think (and just to keep warm). Instead of a "thinking cap", she has a "thinking shawl", or could be said to use it to "collect" herself, wrapping herself up and keeping herself and her thoughts contained.

CHAPTER XI

She conducted me to her own chair, and then began to remove my shawl and untie my bonnet–strings; I begged she would not give herself so much trouble.

On Jane's initial arrival at Thornfield, Mrs. Fairfax removes Jane's shawl, apparently without asking. At first, I thought of this as a servile gesture akin to the lowest servant in a first–century household being the one to wash a newly–arrived guest's filthy feet. On further thought, however, this has a different feel to me. It seems forceful, taking Jane's things instead of asking for them. It also seems rather familiar and perhaps condescending, something an adult would do to a child, an unusual act from someone Jane has just met.

CHAPTER XV

I hurried on my frock and a shawl; I withdrew the bolt and opened the door with a trembling hand.

Leaving her room the night Bertha tries to burn Rochester in his bed, Jane puts on a shawl. She doesn't just put on her dressing gown; she puts on her dress (and whatever undies were necessary, I would imagine). She doesn't just put on her dress; she puts on a shawl, too. I can't imagine taking that much time to get dressed in the middle of a crisis; can you? (I'd be lucky to remember to put on anything!) Was getting dressed, particularly putting on her shawl, Jane's version of putting on her armor before going into battle?

CHAPTER XV

You have a shawl on? If you are not warm enough, you may take my cloak yonder; wrap it about you, and sit down in the arm-chair: there,—I will put it on.

Rochester makes sure Jane is warm (protected) before he goes up to the attic to deal with Bertha after she tries to burn him. This also shows how ubiquitous shawls were for Jane (for all women at that time?) because he immediately verifies his assumption that she is wearing one.

CHAPTER XXIII

He was taking off my shawl in the hall, and shaking the water out of my loosened hair, when Mrs. Fairfax emerged from her room.

Rochester removes Jane's shawl when coming back into the house after proposing to her. This seems to me like a very intimate gesture – taking off her shawl, shaking the water out of her hair. It has a very sensual feel to me; it's easy to imagine them standing there, dripping wet, laughing, bumping into each other as they shake off, his touching her hair to shake out the water. This is as close to disrobing as upright, moral Jane will get without a wedding ring. When Mrs. Fairfax emerges, Jane and Rochester are like a pair of teenagers necking on the doorstep after a date; it's as if they've been caught.

If we see shawls as armor or protection, Rochester's removing her shawl inside his house right after she has accepted his marriage proposal takes on another significance; it as is if he is telling her she no longer needs external protection because he will now be her protector.

CHAPTER XXV

Wrapped up in a shawl, I still carried the unknown little child: I might not lay it down anywhere, however tired were my arms—however much its weight impeded my progress, I must retain it.

Jane's nightmare is very puzzling to me. Who is the child? Is it Jane's newly–born happiness? Is it some fear? Is it Jane's sense of self? Is it her awakening sexuality? Whoever or whatever the child signifies, she does not carry the child in her bare arms, but wrapped up in a shawl: She uses a shawl in this instance, not to protect herself, but someone else. Here, she is the strong one – burdened, but strong nonetheless.

Chapter XXVII

The other articles I made up in a parcel; my purse, containing twenty shillings (it was all I had), I put in my pocket: I tied on my straw bonnet, pinned my shawl, took the parcel and my slippers, which I would not put on yet, and stole from my room.

Again, Jane's shawl is part of the armor she puts on before facing the world – in this case, the wide world as she flees Thornfield, Rochester, the temptations to adultery and bigamy, and the carnal side of her nature that so desperately wants to let her love for Rochester trump her moral, religious scruples.

Chapter XXVIII

I folded my shawl double, and spread it over me for a coverlet; a low, mossy swell was my pillow.

Sleeping on the moor when she has nowhere to go, Jane uses her shawl as a blanket. In this instance, at least, I doubt her shawl was triangular; that would have been less practical as a coverlet. Here, the shawl is both protection – from the cold and wet – and comfort.

Chapter XXIX

My clothes hung loose on me; for I was much wasted, but I covered deficiencies with a shawl, and once more, clean and respectable looking—no speck of the dirt, no trace of the disorder I so hated, and which seemed so to degrade me, left—I crept down a stone staircase with the aid of the banisters, to a narrow low passage, and found my way presently to the kitchen.

When Jane prepares to meet St. John Rivers and his household after her recovery, she hides her "deficiencies" with a shawl, which is a new role for shawls. Again, it can be seen as part of her armor, her protection as she heads out into the unknown, both literally (since she is unfamiliar with the house and how to find the kitchen) and figuratively (not knowing what she has gotten herself into). Are Jane's deficiencies simply the pounds she has lost while ill, or is this a case of the mature Jane projecting current knowledge onto her telling of what happened in the past? Does she say this because, in hindsight, she knows what St. John would have seen as her deficiencies? How do we hide our deficiencies, both real and perceived?

CHAPTER XXXVII

I asked John to go down to the turn-pike-house, where I had dismissed the chaise, and bring my trunk, which I had left there: and then, while I removed my bonnet and shawl, I questioned Mary as to whether I could be accommodated at the Manor House for the night; and finding that arrangements to that effect, though difficult, would not be impossible, I informed her I should stay.

On arriving at Ferndean to return to Mr. Rochester & stay forever, Jane removes her shawl. When she first arrived at Thornfield, Mrs. Fairfax took Jane's shawl away from her, but now Jane removes it herself. What does this say about how Jane has changed and become less passive? Look at the confidence she displays – "I informed her I should stay". She doesn't ask; she tells. This is the last mention of a shawl in the novel. Why does Jane no longer need a shawl? Is it because Rochester is now her protection and warmth or because Jane is now strong enough to be Rochester's protection, his eyes and hand?

— Erica

DOSSIERS

DESIGNERS

BRENDA DAYNE

An experienced rabble–rouser and long–time apple cart upsetter, Brenda Dayne has been writing manifestos since her fifth grade teacher disallowed dancing at recess. A skilled journalist, interviewer, profile and feature writer, she has won international respect work as the creator and host of Cast On – a podcast dedicated to the radical notion that knitting *matters*. A frequent contributor to Interweave Knits and Interweave Crochet, Brenda has interviewed and profiled numerous hand knit designers and artists, traveled widely, and written extensively about the knitting scene in Europe and the UK.

All that Brenda knows about life she learned from her knitting; that there's no right or wrong way to do anything, only different approaches; that gauge is a suggestion, not a Commandment; that it's supposed to be fun.

A native of Portland, Oregon, Brenda now lives with her partner of ten years in a small village in West Wales, where the ale is strong, the people friendly, and news travels fast. Brenda is the mother of two fine young men, one of whom married a nice Welsh girl, and lives nearby, and one who still lives in Portland. She still writes manifestos.

DAWN ELLERD

Dawn is proceeding through stay–at–home–parenthood as a bit of a handicraft dabbler. A serious crochet habit has lately been moderated by judicious amounts of knitting, spinning and hand–loom weaving. There may occasionally be beading. And possibly soap making. Oh yeah, and a lot of foodie–type things. She has written for Interweave Crochet, was a regular columnist for the now–defunct Lime & Violet's Daily Chum website, and is currently designing for Briar Rose Fibers. In general, she is simply shocked silly to find herself somewhere in her 30s as full time caretaker of a menagerie that consists of various little people, English bulldogs and a husband. When spare minutes allow or an avalanche of photos force her to dig out, she blogs irregularly at Crochet Compulsive.

GRETCHEN FUNK

Gretchen Funk and her family live in and love Minnesota. She was introduced to knitting at an early age through trips to the local knit shop with her father, who was an avid knitter. She teaches knitting on both sides of the Mississippi the Yarnery in St Paul and at Crafty Planet in Minneapolis. In addition to teaching, designing, and messing around in all areas of fiber arts, she and her husband own and operate a busy bar with live music and great food called the Triple Rock Social Club. Her designs are available on Ravelry or on the upcoming http://gfunkknits.com.

CHRISSY GARDINER

Chrissy Gardiner began her knitting odyssey in 2005, shortly after the birth of her second child. Finding herself a bit stir crazy at home with an infant and toddler (but with absolutely no desire to go back to her former career as a software architect), she decided to figure out how to turn her craft obsession into a little business. Thus, Gardiner Yarn Works was born.

Chrissy is a regular contributor to Interweave Knits and has designed for Knitty, Twist Collective, Classic Elite Yarns, Blue Moon Fiber Arts and numerous compilation books. She has published her own line of patterns, Gardiner Yarn Works, since 2006 and in 2009 published her first book, *Toe–Up! Patterns and Worksheets to Whip Your Sock Knitting Into Shape*. She is hard at work on her second book, *Indie Socks*, to be published in 2011.

You can find more of Chrissy's work at her website, http://www.gardineryarnworks.com. She blogs occasionally at http://knittinmom.blogspot.com and can be found on Ravelry as chrissyg and on twitter as @knittinmom. She lives in beautiful Portland, Oregon, with her two kids, three cats, two rabbits and one extremely patient husband.

HUNTER HAMMERSEN

Hunter Hammersen is an avid knitter and perpetual student. She harbors the undying hope that when she finally graduates she'll have more time to knit. Read about Hunter's knitting adventures and find her other patterns at www.violently domestic.com. Learn about her first book, *Silk Road Socks: 14 Patterns Inspired by Oriental Rugs* at www. silkroadsocks.com. (Note from Editor: Holy smoke is this book a gazonga!! I got to edit it in text–form and even without the pictures I loved it—and I learned a ton. And now I have 14 more socks I need to knit, plus the ones from this book, plus…)

ERICA HERNANDEZ

Erica lives in "The Birthplace of Biotech" with her husband, daughters Thing One and Thing Two, Pit Bull, and the memory of her son. She learned to knit as a child and, after a 30-year hiatus, picked up needles and yarn again in 2004. Her first project that year was a scarf knit as she mourned the loss of her newborn son. Since then, Erica has rarely been without her knitting, even on a catamaran 50 miles from shore in the Pacific Ocean and in a hotel lounge in Singapore (She doesn't knit during church services, but nearly everywhere else is fair game—Heather likes to believe God would understand).

Erica has been: a test and sample knitter for Wendy Bernard, Chris Church, and Melissa Leapman published in Knitty.com, a first place winner in her local county fair (2006), and has recently branched out into publishing her own designs (and she thinks that all makes her sound much "bigger" than she really is).

She is an avid CraftLit listener, trying to keep the "B.A. in English" portion of her brain from rotting away from disuse. Her previous roles have included stints as a trainee teacher, receptionist, stressed-out LAN administrator, marketing coordinator, website content editor, and more, but she enjoys the at-home mom gig the most. She blogs sporadically and is on Ravelry, Facebook, and Twitter as ericah64.

WENDY McDONNELL

After the birth of her middle child, Wendy took up quilting as a hobby. Being Type A, she went whole hog into quilting and filled the home with fabric. This turned into a small sewing business at WendysModestDress.com. During this time she also did a bit of writing and was published in a few different magazines. When the sewing got to be too much she started to crochet again, which then led to a massive stash of crocheting thread... all the way down to size 70!

After that craze died off a bit Wendy went head first into knitting again (learned as a child), which lead to SABLE (Stash Acquisitition Beyond Life Expectancy) in 6 months! Needless to say, she will be knitting her garage down for a good, long time. Wendy also worked as a professional spinner for a large independent yarn company and has test knit for a dozen or so other companies. Her work has been seen in catalogs, magazines, books and on the catwalk at Stitches West. She prefers the knitting and so remains firmly entrenched in test knitting and designing, but will spin forever because surely it's as good as walking, right? Wendy lives 1 hour from town in the sticks on 2.5 acres with her husband, 2 children, 2 dogs, 2 cats, a pony and a sheep (only one of which is female, her model and youngest child). Since they live so far from the city she learned to spin and dye to cover all her many yarnie needs without ever leaving the house. She did branch out into hand dyeing but found it too all-consuming (that Type A still) and so now only does it to suit the family needs. Wendy worked with Renee of Goddess Knits, the lovely hand dyed

Goddess Lace yarn was enjoyed by many in a just the few KALs but she prefers to dye for personal enjoyment. You can see a few patterns on Ravelry the most popular of which is the Beaded Scallop Smoke Ring cowl. Wendy can be found at wmdress@sbcglobal.net and blogs a bit at http://wmdramble.blogspot.com

JEN MINNIS

J en was afflicted early on with an overwhelming desire to know how make things. This propelled her on a quest to learn and experiment with everything she could get her hands on. Jen's journey has lead through pottery, stone sculpture, bookbinding, paper cutting, egg dying, glass etching, paper making, collage, assemblage, quilting, embroidery, crochet, spinning, knitting, needle felting, pine needle basketry, wood turning, scroll sawing, resin casting, gourd carving, silk painting, quilling, weaving, drawing, painting, polymer clay, printmaking…. and much, much more! Although she has a hard time settling down to any one media, she is best known for her Scherenschnitte (paper cuttings), her Pysanky (dyed eggs), and her resin jewelry featuring her own artwork.

Jen learned to knit from her grandmother as a small girl. After producing one lumpy chunk unappreciated scarf, she set aside her needles and walked away from knitting for the next 25 years. When she rediscovered it and all the wonders it could produce, she dove in and didn't look back. Jen has done test and catalog sample knitting for Knit Picks, SWTC and several independent knitwear designers. She is currently branching out and experimenting with a few of her own designs.

She can be found on Ravelry and Facebook as Esmecat. she can be contacted by email at esmekitten@gmail.com. Her online gallery and her artwork available for purchase can be found through http://www.jenminnis.com and you can always peek at what she's been up to latest at her blog at http://www.jenminnis.com/artblog

SYNE MITCHELL

A nswering the question "How the heck do you do that?" is the focus of Syne's life. Most nights you'll find her experimenting in her studio until the wee hours. (The deer in the forest outside have learned to ignore the green glow). When she's not crafting, Syne writes. Because knowing the answer is only half the fun, you have to share it with others. An award-winning writer with a background in physics, Syne has published five science-fiction novels and has written for Spin-Off; Handwoven; The Journal of Weavers, Spinners and Dyers; Complex Weavers; Shuttle, Spindle and Dyepot, and Knitty. Her column "Weaving the Web" is a regular feature in Handwoven. She produces WeaveZine.com, a website packed with weaving how-to's and tutorials. There you'll also find her blog and podcast. She's on Ravelry as "Syne Mitchell" and @weavezine on Twitter.

Dianne Reade-Jackson

A lover of classic literature and many forms of fiber arts, Dianne learned to knit as a child and has been avidly knitting since 1996. Spinning followed in 2000 and a few years later she was a founding member of the Clear Water Fiber Guild in Western Wisconsin. She is married to a man who won her heart by telling fascinating stories and mother to a grown son who shares her love of reading. Employed in the travel industry since 1980, wherever she travels; yarn, needles and a book are always close at hand.

Kathleen Rogers

K athleen Rogers has been doing needle crafts since way back in the middle of the 20th century when her mother taught her to crochet lace edgings for linen handkerchiefs, as well as to cook, sew, and embroider. She learned to knit from her aunt so that she could make a mustard-yellow sweater (with black and red embroidery) she saw in a magazine. In the 21st century, her color sense has improved, and she loves working with hand-dyed yarns from independent dyers, and with one-of-a-kind yarns from artisanal spinners. She and her knitting and crocheting projects and designs can be found on Ravelry where she is katrog. In real life, she lives with her husband and her craft supplies within earshot of Boston. You can find more of her patterns at her Ravelry store (http://www.ravelry. com/designers/kathleen-rogers).

Meg Warren

M eg is currently living in Italy but the world is truly her home. Having lived in Korea and Japan, in addition to her small Idaho ranch, she has enjoyed travelling the world in an effort to learn as much as she can. Some of her favorite spots are Thailand, Hong Kong, China, Ireland and Wales. She has had some of her artwork exhibited in Tokyo and some of her haiku published there as well as in the United States.

She learned to knit as a child but found the experience to be "sticks in the eyes" frustrating due to the perfectionist attitude taken by her grandmother who told her the only way to fix a problem was to rip back to it. From this she learned to love imperfection in all aspects of her life. When she took knitting back up she discovered that the only thing she remembers from childhood is how her grandmother taught her to hold her needles. So she knits in the old Scottish style…and thanks her grandmother every day of her life for having the patience to try to teach someone so unwilling to learn.

She owns a small yarn business, March Hare Yarns, and until recently raised her own sheep for spinning wool. She knits all the time, everywhere … much to the confusion of her Italian neighbors.

SHANNON OKEY

Shannon Okey is the author of more than a dozen craft–related books, the former editor of Yarn Forward magazine, and a columnist/frequent contributor for many others. She owns and operates Cooperative Press, an innovative publishing company, from her office at Knitgrrl Studio (her teaching space) in a recycled industrial factory building in Cleveland, Ohio. Visit CP online at cooperativepress.com and find Shannon at http://knitgrrl.com (or @knitgrrl on Twitter).

ANDI SMITH

Knitting and reading! What could be more satisfying? Andi loves both and thoroughly enjoyed co-designing Jane Fairfax's Tippet with Shannon. Andi drew on memories of her childhood in Yorkshire and a picture of her great grandmother to co-create this wonderful neck warmer. Andi has been knitting and designing for many years and her work can be seen in a variety of books and magazines as well as on her blog http://www.knitbrit.com.

HEATHER ORDOVER

Heather has been a performative person her whole life (read: ham). Because of this it shouldn't have surprised anyone that she became an award winning University and New York City high school teacher after leaving Hollywood. Where else would she find people willing to pay her to entertain large groups of people—all while telling them what to do? Post–9/11 and the birth of her two boys, she transitioned into writing full time after ~~doing her time~~ — um — ~~serving her country~~ teaching for ten years.

Since leaving the high school classroom she has written online content for Pearson's interactive Focus on Grammar, Teacher's Notes for Scholastic's Literary Cavalcade, and several online masters–level courses in education for online universities. Along with writing for education, Ordover has written and recorded essays for Cast–On: A Podcast for Knitters and currently hosts her own long–running, online podcast, CraftLit: A Podcast for Crafters Who Love Books (think "books on tape with benefits"). Her crafty writing has appeared in Spin–Off, WeaveZine, and The Arizona Daily Star. She currently lives and writes in Tucson, AZ with her loving husband, their two goofy sons, the boy's protective dogs, and a single, mournful, blue–tongued skink.

You can find links to all of the irons in her fire at http://crafting–a–life.com. She is MamaOKnits on Ravelry and MamaO on Twitter

Tech Editors and Stunt Knitters

Alexandra Virgiel

Alexandra is a longtime knitter and designer who has been working as a technical editor since 2005 in both freelance and staff positions for several well-known publications. You can find her online at alexandravirgiel.com, and watch for her upcoming book from Cooperative Press!

Kate Atherley

Kate is Knitty's sock technical editor You can find her online at http://wisehilda.blogspot.com. She also has a book coming out from Cooperative Press in 2011! (What are the odds?)

Kathy Lewinski

Stunt Knitter for Jane's Ubiquitous Shawl—A former indie record–company drone, Kat is a stay–at–home foodie and crafter in Minnesota. When she lived in San Francisco, she was a founding member of the San Francisco Chicks With Sticks group and the window display designer for Noe Knit. Kat and her husband Matt have a foodie blog at http://agoodappetite.blogspot.com. Her varied crafting can be followed at http://kat–knits.blogspot.com, http://theironcraft.blogspot.com, and http://thesnuggery.etsy.com. A designer in her own right, Kat is known as katbaro on Ravelry, where she has more than ten of her own patterns available.

Robbin Hayes

Stunt Knitter for Bertha's Mad Möbius—Robbin is a dedicated Malabrigo Junkie who has test–knit for Nina Machlin Dayton, Tricia Lewis, and Melissa Leapman. She lives and knits in Alameda, CA, surrounded by her patient husband, loving children, and adorable grandson...and a metric ton of Mmmalabrigo. Robbin can be found on Ravelry as knitastic132; if you're looking for her, she'll be on the Malabrigo Junkie boards. Of course.

Toni Markiet

Stunt Knitter for Cthulhu—Toni has been knitting most of her life. She learned embroidery from her mother but they did not see eye to eye on how to hold knitting needles. It was only when Toni met a Norwegian–born friend in college that she was able to learn the Continental method of knitting and became a lifetime devotee. She's knit everything from sweaters, coats, hats, baptism gowns, and now her current love is socks!

ACKNOWLEDGEMENTS

This book wouldn't be in your hands or on your screen without the help and support of a number of people.

First, Zabet Stewart is in many ways the one to thank for the entire project as it was she who introduced me to Shannon Okey. I never dreamt that a relationship with a publisher could be so… so cooperative. Shannon is a wellspring of genius, insight and humor. This book wouldn't be here without her — for more reasons than the ones you're thinking.

Jen Minnis , my co-conspirator, kept my spirits up and made every day feel like Christmas. Getting an email from Jen was the best gift anyone could get as it was always filled with art. Not since I worked at Disney Animation have I seen someone who could produce beauty so fast.

My designers. What an extraordinary group of fiber artists. Some are being introduced to the world of pattern publishing for the first time and I'm proud to be the one to bring them out. I'm especially proud of how Shannon and I structured the making of the book. Each designer has a share in it. They were paid nothing up front and guaranteed nothing at the end but a share in any profits. If you like the book, please tell a friend to buy it. Cooperative Press isn't The-Man-Who-You-Want-To-Stick-It-To by photocopying the patterns for friends — Shannon and I both felt strongly that designers should be compensated for their work like the professionals they are.

And finally, I need to think the people who helped me see that this wicked crazy idea was really a good one: my mother Barbara, my father Charles, my in-laws Abe and Eleanor, and my uncle-in-law Buddy. Their support went beyond the financial and entered the realm of inspirational. You wouldn't be holding this book without their aid. Cousins Mark and Steve who, sitting in a pool in Mexico, showed me that I wasn't crazy and that I could start Crafting–a–Life.com which gave birth to this book. And finally and most importantly, my husband and sons. Andrew's belief in me never faltered and his patience with my distractedness proves he is what his mother and I always knew he was: a real mensch. And my two boys who always understood what I was doing and were happy to ply me with hugs then flop on a table in my workroom and start creating their own art — I love you all more than I can say.

Thank you, all.

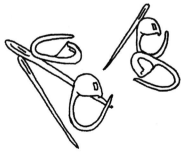

PATTERN RESOURCES

Links to purchasable print copies of all inspirational texts can be found at: http://astore. amazon.com/crapofocrwhlo-20?_encoding=UTF8&node=3 and all links here are live at http://crafting-a-life/wwmdfk/links so you do not need to retype each one yourself. The links will be updated or revised as time goes by to ensure continued access. If you find a broken link, please don't hesitate to contact us.

JANE'S UBIQUITOUS SHAWL
Jane Eyre (audio) available on librivox.org

PRINCESS LANGWIDERE
Inspiration for the lace pattern: "Holland Lace" from *A Treasury of Knitting Patterns* by Barbara Walker
Ozma of Oz (audio) available on librivox.org

NOT-SO-RUBY SLIPPERS AND MONKEY MINIONS
Wizard of Oz (audio) available on librivox.org

ISOLDE, TRISTAN, VAN TASSEL
CraftLit's Tristan & Isolde and "Sleepy Hollow" episodes (audio)
crafting–a–life.com/craftlit/?page_id=1394

MERMAID LAGOON
Peter Pan (audio) available on librivox.org

HYDE'S HOODED SWEATER
CraftLit's Jekyll and Hyde episodes (audio)
crafting–a–life.com/craftlit/?page_id=1401

BERTHA'S MAD MÖBIUS
Wide Sargasso Sea by Jean Rhys New York, W.W. Norton & Company, 1982 (paperback)

FLATLAND COLOUR REVOLT
CraftLit's *Flatland* episodes (audio) crafting–a–life.com/craftlit/?page_id=1405

CTHULHU WAITS
Cthulhu Podcast (audio) cthulhupodcast.blogspot.com/2008_04_01_archive.html

AHAB'S SCARF
Moby Dick (audio) librivox.org/moby–dick–by–herman–melville

FRANKENHOOD
Frankenstein by Mary Wollstonecraft Shelley, the inspiration behind the pattern.

Fashion Geek by Diana Eng, a book of eTextile techniques and patterns.

The following websites sell eTextile supplies:
* Sparkfun (conductive thread, LEDs, and more), www.sparkfun.com
* Aniomagic (LED sequins, eTextile kits, etc), www.aniomagic.com
* Radio Shack (LEDs, coin batteries and holders), www.radioshack.com

WOLF-SLAYER
From *Grimm's Household Tales*, volume 1 by The Brothers Grimm (1812), translated from the German and edited by Margaret Hunt (1884). The English version of this story, the well-known Little Red Riding Hood, is probably derived more immediately from the French, 'Le Petit Chaperon Rouge,' as given by Perrault, where it ends with the death of the girl.

ANCIENT MARINER WATCH CAP
CraftLit's "Rime of the Ancient Mariner" episode (audio)
crafting-a-life.com/craftlit/?cat=18
Yarn source: Yellow Dog Knitting www.yellowdogknitting.com

GLACIAL GAUNTLET
A Doll's House (audio) available on librivox.org

MS PRYNNE
* *The Scarlet Letter* by Nathaniel Hawthorne. Many print editions are available, or listen at CraftLit: A Free Podcast for Crafters who Love Books (www.craftlit.com)
* *Knit and Crochet with Beads* by Lily Chin. Loveland, Colorado: Interweave Press, 2004. Many beading techniques and patterns employing each, also includes a chapter on designing your own projects.
* Sivia Harding Knit Design (www.siviaharding.com). An array of instructional patterns for lace and other beaded projects. Free patterns and techniques section.
* Beads for knitting are available from www.earthfaire.com

WILHELMINA
Dracula (audio) available on librivox.org

DEFARGE STOLE
CraftLit's *Tale of Two Cities* episodes (audio) crafting-a-life.com/craftlit/?page_id=1392

LYSISTRATA'S CHITON
Lysistrata (audio) available on librivox.org

JANE FAIRFAX'S TIPPET
Emma (audio) available on librivox.org

STITCH GLOSSARY

CROCHET PROVISIONAL CAST ON

With waste yarn, make a chain for the number of sts you need to cast on. Fasten off. Tie a knot in the tail so you know which end to unravel from later. With knitting needle and main yarn, pick up and knit 1 st in each "bump" along the backside of the chain. To unzip the cast on later, find the end with the knotted tail, pick out the fastened-off chain, and pull on the tail to unravel.

FOUNDATION SINGLE (DOUBLE, ETC.) CROCHET

Foundation crochet is a way of creating the initial chain and working the first row of single crochet (or double, or half-double...) at the same time. It makes a stable edge.

To begin, ch2. Insert hook under top two strands of first ch and pull up a loop. Yo, pull through 1 loop. This creates the chain part of the stitch. Yo, pull through 2 loops. This is the single crochet part. *Insert hook in left and back loops of previous chain. Yo, pull through 1 loop. Yo, pull through 2 loops. Repeat from *.

To work foundation half double crochet:
Ch2. Yo, insert hook under top two strands of first ch and pull up a loop. Yo, pull through 1 loop. Yo, pull through all 3 loops. *Insert hook in left and back loops of previous chain. Yo, pull through 1 loop. Yo, pull through 3 loops. Repeat from *.

Foundation double crochet:
Ch2. Yo, insert hook under top two strands of first ch and pull up a loop. Yo, pull through 1 loop. [Yo, pull through 2 loops] twice. *Insert hook in left and back loops of previous chain. Yo, pull through 1 loop. [Yo, pull through 2 loops] twice. Repeat from *.

THREE-NEEDLE BIND OFF

Have the two sets of stitches to be joined on separate needles, held parallel with wrong sides facing. Insert a third needle into first st on front needle, then first st on back needle and knit together as if they were one st. *Insert third needle into next st on front needle, then next st on back needle and knit together as if they were one st. Pass first st on right-hand needle over second and off needle to bind off 1 st. Repeat from * until all sts are bound off.

MAKING TASSELS

See page 130 for basic tassel instructions that can be applied to any project, or page 195 for visual instructions.

CHART SYMBOLS

BASIC STITCHES		
	No stitch RS: placeholder, no st made
	Knit RS: knit WS: purl
B *alternately:* |	**knit tbl** RS: knit st through back loop WS: purl st through back loop
●	**purl** RS: purl st WS: knit st
~	**purl tbl** RS: purl st through back loop WS: knit st through back loop
C	**Corner stitch** RS: knit
⦂	**purl, knit, purl** RS: (purl, knit, purl) into same st
*	**p1, drop 1** RS: purl into 1st loop of double YO from previous row, drop 2nd loop

SLIPPED STITCHES		
V	**slip** RS: sl st as if to p, holding yarn in back WS: sl st as if to p, holding yarn in back
V̲	**slip wyif** RS: slip st as if to p, with yarn in front WS: slip st as if to p, with yarn in back
λ̄	**sl 1 kwise k1 psso** RS: sl 1 as if to k, k 1 st, pass slipped st over
λ	**sl1 k psso** RS: sl 1, k 1, pass slipped st over
Λ	**sl 1 k2tog psso** RS: sl 1, k2tog, pass slipped st over k2tog
\	**ssk** RS: sl 1 st as if to knit, sl another knitwise, insert left needle into front of these sts, k tog WS: p 2 sts tog in back loops, inserting needle from behind and into the backs of the 2nd and 1st sts in that order

INCREASES	
M	**Make one** RS: lift strand in between st just worked and next st, k into back of this strand WS: same, but p into back of strand
MR	**Make one right** RS: Place a firm backward loop over R needle so yarn end goes towards back WS: Place a firm backward loop over R needle so yarn end goes towards front
ML	**Make one left** RS: Place a firm backward loop over R needle so yarn end goes towards front WS: Place a firm backward loop over R needle so yarn end goes towards back
Y	**Kfb** RS: k into the front and back of the st RS: p into the front and back of the st
O	**YO** RS: yarn over WS: same
②	**YO twice** RS: yarn over twice WS: same

DECREASES	
╱	**k2tog** RS: k 2 sts tog WS: purl 2 sts tog
⟍	**k2tog tbl** RS: k 2 sts tog through back loop WS: p 2 sts tog through back loop
╱╲	**k3 tog** RS: k 3 sts tog as 1 WS: p 3 sts tog as 1
✕	**Bind off 1 st**
╱.	**p2tog** RS: p 2 sts tog WS: k 2 sts tog
╲.	**p2tog tbl** RS: p 2 sts tog in back loops, inserting needle from the left, behind and into the backs for the 2nd and 1st sts in that order WS: sl 1 st as if to knit, slip a second st knitwise, insert left hand needle into front of these 2 sts and k them tog

UNUSUAL STITCH:

 twisted raised inc: RS: k into back of st in row below, twisted

∧	**Central Double Decrease** RS: sl 1st and 2nd sts as if to k; k one st, pass 2 slipped sts over the k st WS: Slip 1st and 2nd sts together as if to p through the back loop; p one st, pass 2 slipped sts over the p st
CABLE STITCHES	
	c1 twisted knit over 1 purl right RS: sl 1 to CN, hold CN to back, k 1 tbl, p1 from CN
	c1 twisted knit over 1 purl left RS: sl 1 to CN, hold CN to front, p1, k 1 tbl from CN
	c1 over 2 right RS: sl 2 to CN, hold in back. k1, k2 from CN
	c1 over 2 left RS: sl 1 to CN, hold CN to back, k1 tbl, k1 from CN
	c1 twisted knit over 1 knit right RS: sl 1 to CN, hold CN to back, k1 tbl, k1 from CN

	c1 twisted knit over 1 knit left RS: sl 1 to CN, hold CN to front, k1, k1 tbl from CN
	c1 twisted knit over 2 knit right RS: sl 2 to CN, hold CN to back, k1 tbl, k2 from CN
	c1 twisted knit over 1 twisted knit right RS: sl 1 to CN, hold CN to back, k1 tbl, k1 tbl from CN
	c1 twisted knit over 1 twisted knit left RS: sl 1 to CN, hold CN to front, k1 tbl, k1 tbl from CN
	c1 twisted knit over 2 knit left RS: sl 1 to CN, hold CN to front, k2, k1 tbl from CN
	c1 twisted knit over 2 purl right RS: sl 2 to CN, hold CN to back, k1 tbl, p2 from CN
	c1 twisted knit over 2 purl left RS: sl 1 to CN, hold CN to front, p2, k1 tbl from CN

⊟	**double twist** RS: twist next st on needle then k tbl
⅄⅄	**Right twist** RS: Skip 1st st, knit into 2nd st, then k skipped st. Sl both sts from needle together OR k2tog, leaving sts on LH needle, then k first st again, slip both sts off needle WS: Skip first st, p second st, then p the skipped st. Slip both sts from needle together
⅄⅄	**Left twist** Skip 1st st, knit into back of 2nd st, then knit slipped st. Sl both sts from needle together.
⅄⅄	**c2 over 2 right** RS: sl 2 to CN, hold in back. k2, k2 from CN
⅄⅄	**c2 over 2 left** RS: sl 2 to CN, hold in front. k2, k2 from CN
<-③--->	**6 st wrap** RS: with yarn in back, sl next 6 sts to RH needle, move yarn to front, sl 6 sts back to LH needle (repeat twice) there will be 3 wraps around the 6 sts, then knit them.

TASSELS
a quick visual primer

If you're a visual learner, this may help you more than the directions on page 130.

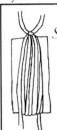 *Step 1:* Cut a cardboard scrap the desired length of your tassel and wrap yarn around it until you reach the desired thickness. Wrap another piece of yarn around one end and tie tightly.

 *Step 4:* Slip the end of the yarn through the loop.

 *Step 2:* Cut the other end of the wrapped yarn. With one of the pieces, form a loop and lay it against the tassel.

 *Step 5:* Pull the short end of the yarn, drawing the loop and other end of the yarn under the collar.

 *Step 3:* Holding the short end of the loop firmly in place, wrap the yarn tightly around the bundle, forming a collar.

Step 6: Trim ends and fluff tassel. Enjoy!

INDEX BY PATTERN TYPE

If you're searching for your next project by type, this quick cross-reference should help you find just the right pattern.

TOYS

The Mermaid's Lagoon (page 54)
Winged Monkey Minions (page 119)

CROCHET

Not-so-Ruby Slippers (page 29)
Colour Revolt Triangular Shawl(ette) (page 89)
Winged Monkey Minions (page 119)
Wolf Slayer (page 129)

WHY, MR DICKENS!

things unavailable in Charles' day that you may find helpful

Using your smartphone or other QR-reader enabled device, scan this code to go directly to the WWMDfK? website, where you will find the most current versions of links relating to these patterns, errata (if any) and much more.

No smartphone? Do it the "old-fashioned way" and visit:

WWMDFK.COM

ABOUT COOPERATIVE PRESS
partners in publishing

Cooperative Press (*formerly anezka media*) was founded in 2007 by Shannon Okey, a voracious reader as well as writer and editor, who had been doing freelance acquisitions work, introducing authors with projects she believed in to editors at various publishers.

Although working with traditional publishers can be very rewarding, there are some books that fly under their radar. They're too avant-garde, or the marketing department doesn't know how to sell them, or they don't think they'll sell 50,000 copies in a year.

5,000 or 50,000. Does the book *matter* to that 5,000? Then it should be published.

In 2009, Cooperative Press changed its named to reflect the relationships we have developed with authors working on books. We work together to put out the best quality books we can and share in the proceeds accordingly.

Thank you for supporting independent publishers and authors.

COOPERATIVEPRESS.COM

CPSIA information can be obtained at www.ICGtesting.com
Printed in the USA
BVOW012001230712

295968BV00006B/2/P